W9-BVF-791

Birds of the Northern Forest

J. F. LANSDOWNE

WITH

JOHN A. LIVINGSTON

Birds of the Northern Forest

MCCLELLAND AND STEWART

0-7710-4688-X

THE CANADIAN PUBLISHERS
McClelland and Stewart Limited,
25 Hollinger Road, Toronto,
Ontario, Canada

PRINTED AND BOUND IN GREAT BRITAIN

Contents

Introduction

A SUBSTANTIAL part of Canada is forested, and the greater part of that forest consists of cone-bearing evergreens. When most of us speak of "the North" we do not usually mean the arctic – that remote fastness scarcely occurs to any of us – but we do mean the vast expanse of spruce, fir, and larch that lies between us and the truly northern regions. The northern forest we think of is the harsh and exacting land of moose, otter, and red squirrel, of lynx and snowshoe hare. It is a land of insects. It is also the land of the fifty-six species of birds presented in this volume. If Canada can be said to have characteristic birds, they are these.

But the northern forest is not uniquely Canadian, or even North American. If you were to look down on the globe, viewing it from above the north pole, you would see (ignoring water masses) a series of concentric circles. The bull's eye in the middle is the polar ice cap. It is ringed by the wide and treeless tundra. Immediately to the south of the barren grounds is suspended the great mantle of evergreen woods, the northern forest of this book.

Since the huge coniferous blanket is essentially the same in both Eurasia and America, it is not surprising that the two land masses have many of the same forms of wildlife. Bears, wolves, moose, and weasels are common to both. Siberia and Scandinavia are not too radically different from Canada; twenty-one of the birds appearing in this book occur in the Old World (one of them, the Canada goose, was introduced). Some, like the winter wren and the gray-cheeked thrush, made their way into Asia from North America. Others, shrike and kinglets among them, reversed the process, and were immigrants. For an animal with wings, the Bering Strait is no great challenge. In addition to the twenty-one circumpolar species, several more in this book have very closely related "opposite numbers" living in the Old World in much the same way.

In Canada, the northern forest extends from the edge of the barrens south to central Alberta and Saskatchewan, the north shore of Lake Superior, the Gaspé peninsula, and the northern tip of Newfoundland. At its southern fringe in the Great Lakes region and the Maritimes, there is a mixed forest of evergreens and broad-leafed trees which blends the coniferous belt with the hardwood zone of the south. Still farther south, in areas such as Appalachia, elevation has much the same effect as latitude, and stands of evergreens extend the "northern" forest deep into the eastern United States. In the west, the high mountains carry a similar and related cover of cone-bearing trees, and support many of the same birds.

The coniferous woodland roughly parallels the southern limits of Ice Age glaciation. It is the most recent area to have become treed following the retreat of the Pleistocene ice sheet. The north woods support the fewest species of plants and wildlife of any Canadian region with the exception of the arctic, which is still in the process of escaping the glaciers. In comparison with the south, relatively few animals have yet invaded the northern forest. There is a general uniformity in terms of habitat; if an animal likes a handful of evergreen species, that is one thing; if it must have a broad and rich selection of leafy hardwoods then it cannot live in the north.

But even here, in a land that seems nothing but one great stand of conifers, there are different environmental opportunities within the more general habitat, and different kinds of birds have taken advantage of them. The northernmost tree-line with its impoverished vegetation has its special nesting birds, such as the gray-cheeked thrush and the blackpoll warbler. The denser forest is the haunt of owls and spruce grouse. In cool bogs you find the solitary sandpiper, rusty blackbird, and palm warbler. Where fire or flood have opened the forest and begun to promote the growth of aspen, birch, and other deciduous trees, birds such as the lesser yellowlegs and purple finch move in. The lake country is the home of loons, mergansers, and ospreys. The forest is extensive, but it is varied; its birds reflect that variety in the ways in which they have become adapted for existence there.

Not all of the following fifty-six birds are restricted to the northern forest to the exclusion of other habitats. Birds such as the peregrine falcon, the osprey, and the raven are almost cosmopolitan; in Canada, they are found chiefly in the evergreen forest. This is extreme and demanding country, and the summers are short. Many birds of the area are forced to migrate – flycatchers, thrushes, vireos, and warblers among them. They nest in the north, but winter in tropic America. Others stay in the higher latitudes much of the time, but occasionally move south in great numbers according to fluctuations in their food supply. If their populations build up to a point where the local environment can no longer support them, chickadees, several finches, and others will leave the northern forest in some winters for the better possibilities offered by more southern regions. A few species, for example the gray jay, desert the evergreen forest only on very rare occasions.

As a result, many of the birds in this volume are familiar to most Canadians only as spring and fall migrants or occasional winter visitors. Others are best known to wilderness campers, canoe-trippers, and those who have summer cottages in the spruce country. Most are quite widely distributed in Canada, and can be seen fairly predictably at the appropriate seasons. Only one or two, such as the great gray and boreal owls, are "rare," and even they can be encountered from time to time. Their "rarity" is probably a matter of their being thinly distributed over an enormous wilderness area, and of their normally sedentary nature.

Though none of the birds included here is rare in the strict sense, some have endured lamentable population losses in recent times. Since it is impossible, we believe, to be even casually interested in birds without a concomitant interest in their welfare, it is also impossible to prepare a book about birds without reference to their conservation.

The word "conservation" means many things to many people. It is used frequently as a synonym for "wise use" – though we are not altogether sure what *that* means, either. The word seems to convey whatever the user wants it to. "Conservation" is commonly used by the forest industry, for example, to describe its minimal gestures toward the restoration of the resource it has so sadly mutilated – especially on the Pacific coast. It is almost as commonly used by organized fishing and shooting groups to justify such activities as the poisoning of water systems so that a pure culture of some exotic game fish may replace the diverse and wonderful natural community of fishes that developed there. The name of conservation is invoked in connection with the fervently righteous slaughter of crows and magpies. Self-perpetuating government "predator control" agencies poison wolves and coyotes and destroy bears and cougars in the name of "conservation." The word has lost its meaning.

But conservation the ethic – the state of mind – is very much alive. Some people have it; some haven't. Happily, more have it today than did a generation ago. This is due in major degree to the work of such national organizations as the Canadian Audubon Society and other private groups and government agencies at national, provincial, and local levels.

If we are not precisely sure what "conservation" means any more, we do know, however, what "preservation" means, and we do not blush to say that we are preservationists. We believe that the preservation of birds – *all* birds – is a legitimate aim that does not need justification on economic or any other grounds. Birds should be preserved because they are there – because they happened. That, to us, is reason enough.

How the peregrine falcon and the osprey are to be preserved from the insidious chronic effects of chemical pesticides, we do not pretend to know.

Probably it will involve legislative bans on the most lethal compounds and insistence upon the use of non-residual materials. Neither do we really know how to preserve the loon from the deafening, stinking invasion of its forest lakes by the outboard motorboat. You cannot legislate engines out of existence; perhaps we will have sufficient foresight and wisdom to legislate sufficient nature preserves *into* existence.

But we do think we know how to preserve the great gray owl and the hooded merganser from the farm boy with the .22 rifle. That is why we do not hesitate to add one more volume to the already great store of books about our native birds. The greater the number and variety and form and availability of books on birds, the greater the chances of at least some information – and hopefully some inspiration – reaching the right destination. That is sufficient motive in itself for doing another book on birds.

In the three thousand million (or so) years of life on this earth, an awe-inspiring multitude of complex organisms has arisen in response to the opportunities offered by an infinite number of changing environmental conditions. These organisms are specialists. Some convert radiant energy into plant material. Some convert plant material into animal protein. Others convert animal protein into yet another animal protein. They do it in as many different ways as there are different kinds of organisms. In the bird world, there are between eight and nine thousand distinct species, each one unique, each exploiting its environment in a separate, individual way. Even the least of these, in its uniqueness, is irreplaceable both in terms of science and in terms of the maturing conscience of man. Our current sovereignty over much of the living world carries with it a profound responsibility.

Most birds and other wildlife suffer most severely not from overt aggression against them, but from rapid alteration or disruption of their natural environments. Animals are inextricably adjusted to the particular kinds of places they live in; most of them can live nowhere else. Polluted water, levelled woodlots, burned grasslands, and drained marshes all eliminate the special wildlife of each type of area as surely as any conscious campaign of liquidation. But habitat change, though it does occur locally, has not yet affected the bulk of the northern forest. No doubt it will in due course, but at the moment most of the birds in this book (with critical exceptions) are among those least affected by man's gradual scouring of the face of North America.

There are many more than fifty-six species of birds in the northern forest, and thus any selection must be arbitrary. We have tried to include a representative collection of the *kinds* of birds to be found there, and to spread our selection as evenly as possible across the spectrum of the families of northern birds and the varieties of habitat to be found within the region as a whole.

The result of our selection is eleven water birds, nine hawks and owls, thirty-one songbirds, and five miscellaneous species not allied to the others. We consider it a reasonable sample, but only a sample, of the birdlife of the northern forest. If the reader regrets the absence of a favourite species, chances are that it will appear in a future volume of this series of books. Our plan is to deal similarly with other major Canadian environments, such as the eastern hardwood forests, the prairies, the sea coasts, the mountains, the arctic, etc.

The birds are presented in systematic order – loons to sparrows – according to what is generally agreed to be their evolutionary sequence. Finches are thought to have evolved more recently than loons and grebes. (Birds are such perishable, soft-boned creatures, however, that the fossil record of ornithology is regrettably slim.) The order and the nomenclature are those of the 1957 *Check-list of North American Birds* published by the American Ornithologists' Union.

In dealing with a collection of birds ranging in bulk from geese to kinglets, it is clearly impossible to illustrate them in relative size. A book that could accomodate a life-size warbler would run into difficulty with a loon. Accordingly, as a guide, the length in *inches* of each species is provided in a footnote. In the case of hawks, where wingspread is important to identification, that is indicated in *feet*.

The birds were painted from skins loaned to the artist from the large and representative collections of the Royal Ontario Museum in Toronto. James L. Baillie of the ROM's Department of Birds, to whom the author has a lifelong indebtedness for inspiration, guidance, and instruction, has devoted countless hours and days to the selection of bird skins for the artist's reference over many years. Since these are portraits of actual birds that once were living, accompanying each plate for which the data are available there is a note of the place and month of capture. Both are significant to the bird student, and we feel that this additional information will be interesting also to both residents and visitors in the regions concerned.

In many species of birds, the sexes are distinctly different in pattern and coloration. In others, they are to all intents and purposes identical. In still others, the sexes are distinguishable in the field, but there is sufficient similarity between the two that identification of the species is not in doubt. This has guided the artist throughout. The Tennessee warbler is a good example; it was not considered necessary to illustrate the female, even though she is not precisely like the male. The "family" resemblance is sufficient.

The text is not formalized under standard sub-headings for each species (description, field marks, distribution, habits, nest, eggs, etc.). This information is available from a long list of sources in the rich and exhaustive bird literature, a small selection from which is presented in a brief bibliography. Of course it is the fact of this literature, the product of countless field observers and laboratory workers, writers, and artists, to which this book owes its existence. The interdependence of bird students and naturalists generally is just as vital as the interdependence of the wildlife community itself.

The aim of the text has been to point out merely a few interesting or noteworthy points about each bird or group of birds, in the hope that the result will be not only a somewhat closer acquaintance with the species selected and their forest home, but also some appreciation of the nature of birds in general, and the pleasure and wonder that artist and author have derived from them since boyhood.

We love birds. We love painting them, writing and talking about them, watching them and listening to them, and attempting to learn something about them. That is really what this book is all about.

It is dedicated to Budd.

JOHN A. LIVINGSTON

J. F. LANSDOWNE

Birds of the Northern Forest

1

Common Loon

GAVIA IMMER

plate 1

Common Loon - GAVIA IMMER

THERE have been loons of one kind or another in the world for at least sixty million years. They are thought to be the most ancient of Canadian birds; this seniority places them first on our list. For convenience, students arrange birds in sequence from the most "primitive" (those with the oldest fossil record) to those thought to be the most recently evolved – in Canada's case the finches, ending with the longspurs and the snow bunting. This in no sense means that the loon is a simple organism. It is one of the world's more sophisticated animals, superbly adapted to getting a living in the water.

You could imagine that the loon was deliberately designed as a fish-catching machine. It has a projectile-shaped body, strong propulsive feet mounted well to the rear, remarkable vision, and a javelin-like bill, all of which add up to awesome efficiency. It can stay submerged for three minutes or more, and can dive to depths of two hundred feet. Elaborate physiological processes conserve oxygen. Also, it can alter its specific gravity at will, sinking into the water like a submarine until only its head is showing. This is possible because it has relatively solid bones for a bird, and it is able to press air from its lungs, plumage, and elsewhere to give it the desired level of buoyancy.

But if an animal wants to specialize, it cannot have everything, and to achieve such fine adjustments to the water, the loon had to sacrifice some things. One of these was mobility on land. Its legs are set so far back on its body that the bird can scarcely move, and is forced to hump itself along, seal-like, on its breast and belly, or to use its wings as props.

The process of adaptation is mostly a matter of give and take. Large appendages would only get in the way under water, so evolution has drastically cut down on the loon's wing. The result is evident when the heavy, goose-sized bird takes off; it has to taxi quite a distance to become airborne, and once aloft must beat its wings very rapidly to maintain altitude. Like a stubby-winged aircraft, it substitutes power for "lift" area. It cannot take off at all from land. Descent has similar problems; there is no grace in the loon's return to the water. Its small wings allow no hovering and little braking, and the bird sets down in a shallow, inelegant crash-glide with water flying wildly in all directions.

The voice of the common loon, like "woman wailing for her demon lover," is an unforgettable, spine-tingling feature of the northern forest. Its weird yodels and *tremulo* cries are especially stirring after nightfall, when the air is still.

Where they can find seclusion from the increasingly ubiquitous outboard motorboat (bane of the lake country and its wildlife), loons breed throughout the northern part of the northern hemisphere. There are four species, all of which occur in Canada.

Length 28-36 inches. Female, Kamloops, British Columbia, April.

2

Horned Grebe

PODICEPS AURITUS

plate 2

Horned Grebe - PODICEPS AURITUS

ALTHOUGH grebes look and behave superficially like loons, the two are not related. This pint-sized species is known in Britain as the Slavonian grebe; its "horns" are erectile golden feathers which both sexes display in their mutual courtship ceremonies.

Like those of loons, grebes' legs are set very far back on the body for maximum driving power under water, but the feet are totally different. A loon's feet are webbed; a grebe has separate, extraordinarily lobate toes, which give plenty of area for thrust when pushing backward. On the return stroke, the foot folds to ruler-edge thinness to avoid water resistance as much as possible. Grebes are expert divers and underwater hunters, and have all the appropriate physiological as well as anatomical specializations. When they are swimming on the surface, they can regulate the amount of body area that shows above the water. Because of their relatively small wings, grebes are not graceful fliers, but by means of rapid strokes and sheer power manage a reasonable turn of speed.

The nest of a grebe is noteworthy. It consists of a floating, tangled heap of marsh vegetation artlessly thrown together, often anchored to standing water plants. Sometimes it becomes sheltered in the course of incubation by the rapid early-summer growth of adjacent green shoots. Often the whole soggy mass is quite wet, including the eggs, which are covered by a few strands of vegetable matter when the bird leaves the nest.

Young grebes are vividly striped and fuzzy, and look quite unlike their elders. They can swim at birth, but when they are very small they commonly ride about on one of their parents. They mount the adult bird from the rear, make their way along its back and pop into a soft "pocket" under the old bird's wing.

Canada has five grebes, the world, twenty. This species is to be found almost countrywide.

Length 12-15 inches. Male, Lake St. Martin, Manitoba, June.

3

Canada Goose

BRANTA CANADENSIS

Canada Goose - BRANTA CANADENSIS

THE big gray "honker" is unquestionably the most storied and honoured of Canadian waterfowl. In fact it has a world reputation for sagacity, fidelity, altruism, and related manners and motives bordering on the incredible. It is a splendid bird regardless; the anthropomorphic and uncritical legends were spawned by men, not geese.

The Canada goose has been "broken down" by students into nine or ten different races, or subspecies. These range from the small, duck-sized, three-pound version in Alaska to a huge prairie form which may weigh eighteen pounds or more. It is interesting that these several varieties maintain their identities; no doubt they resulted from and are perpetuated by the bird's seemingly unalterable traditional behaviour. Its habit of returning as a family unit to the same nesting grounds year after year apparently promotes enough in-breeding to keep the various populations undiluted genetically.

In spring migration, the northward advance of the geese is exquisitely tied to the thermometer. The birds may be expected to follow immediately in the wake of the 35° isotherm as it moves up the continent in March and April, bringing them to the nesting grounds at virtually the moment after ice break-up.

Canada geese breed when they are two years old and appear to mate for life. If one partner is lost, the survivor remates. Although they are very sociable and gregarious in the off-season, they do not like too much crowding at nesting time, and they demand a certain degree of "elbow-room" from others of their kind.

In common with loons, ducks, and others, geese in the summer moult lose all their flight feathers simultaneously (most birds do not), and are grounded for about three weeks when the young are still half-grown. The very nicely timed result is that both young and adults take to the wing at about the same date.

Numbers of Canada geese appear to remain fairly stable. Despite their popularity with gunners, the geese have been fortunate in the remoteness of their breeding grounds and the usual freedom of these areas from drought. Losses in the shooting season are normally replaced next summer with gratifying regularity – or they have been so far.

Length 22-42 inches. Male.

4

Lesser Scaup

AYTHYA AFFINIS

Lesser Scaup - AYTHYA AFFINIS

THE vernacular name of this duck is a bastardization of the word "scalp." This in turn is related to "scallop" and the shellfish and other invertebrates upon which flocks of scaups feed at low tide, when many of them move to the sea coasts for the winter.

Lesser scaups are known to the duck shooters as "bluebills." They are among the most abundant species of the western continental flyways. Their breeding success is partly due to the fact that they are northern nesters, and thus they are not affected to too great an extent by seasonal droughts and the gradual but inexorable dropping of the prairie water table. They nest late in the season and begin their autumn migration only just ahead of the changing weather.

Their preferred nesting sites are the borders of ponds and freshwater marshes. The nest is a depression in the grass, lined with down which the hen plucks from her breast. Like most ducks, the male deserts the female when the full clutch of nine to twelve buffy-olive eggs has been laid and incubation begins. He moves to a larger body of water, there to flock with other males and wait for the flightless moult period in safety from land predators. Back at the nest, the female has to depend on her camouflaging plumage.

The peculiar laterally-compressed shape of a duck's head, and the unusually high placement of its eyes, are for a very good purpose. Ducks have a range of binocular vision, not only to the front, but also to the rear. Everyone knows how difficult it is to surprise a duck, though lesser scaups can become among the more confiding of their family when encouraged by artificial feeding.

This species is distinguished from the closely related and very similar greater scaup (an Old World as well as North American bird) by the purplish head of the male, its slight crest, and, when in flight, by a relatively short white wing stripe. The greater scaup has a round, green-glossed head and a longer white stripe in the wing.

Length 15-18½ inches. Male, Niagara Falls, Ontario, April.
Female, Niagara Falls, Ontario, April.

5

Common Goldeneye

BUCEPHALA CLANGULA

Common Goldeneye - BUCEPHALA CLANGULA

THE goldeneye is known as a "sea duck," although it breeds on fresh-water lakes in the forested area of Canada and Alaska. Gunners have nicknamed it "whistler" for the distinctive sound delivered by its stiffly vibrating wing feathers.

This is a particularly hardy bird; it is no stranger to cold. In spring, migrating flocks of goldeneyes follow close upon the break-up of ice, and move into lakes and rivers the very moment they are even partially open.

Unlike a great many ducks, the goldeneye does not breed until it is more than one year old. Nesting is in a cavity in a tree, as much as fifty feet from the ground, often some distance from water. The hole is lined with down. After the clutch of eight to twelve greenish-white eggs has been laid, the male departs. The brood hatches in about twenty days, whereupon the downy youngsters are faced with their first major decision in life: how to get to the ground.

They seem to manage this successfully, judging by the numbers of goldeneyes, but just how they do it has long been debated. It has been said that the hen bird may transport the chicks by means of her bill, her back, or her feet. It seems more likely that they simply tumble out and take their chances. Since a little blob of duckling does not weigh much more than the equivalent volume of thistle down, it seems doubtful that many are seriously injured.

With the approach of winter, goldeneyes move only as far south as they absolutely have to. Great rafts concentrate at the southern edges of the ice. If water is open inland, the birds will remain there, but in most winters they are gradually forced toward the coast as the fresh waters close up.

The goldeneye eats a wide variety of food, including mussels, aquatic insects, and the shoots and roots of water plants.

Length 17-23 inches. Female, Niagara Falls, Ontario, May.

6

White-winged Scoter

MELANITTA DEGLANDI

White-winged Scoter - MELANITTA DEGLANDI

IN swimming and diving, different water birds use different techniques. Penguins, for example, literally fly under water, propelling themselves with their wings, using the feet to assist in steering. Scoters do it the other way round. Propulsion is with the feet, and the wings seem to serve as rudders.

Notice in the plate the way in which the bird's wings are raised away from the body somewhat, with their tips crossed over the tail. At the wrist, a thumb-like "bastard wing" called the *alula* is extended away at an angle from the rest of the wing. This may be a particularly specialized underwater propulsive device, or it may act as a stabilizer. The alula is present in all birds, but its use in this way is especially noticeable in the scoters.

The bird pictured is a female. The male white-winged scoter is velvety-black with the same white patch at the rear edge of the wing, and a brilliant orange bill. Like the goldeneye, this species emits a peculiar whistling note which is thought to be produced by the wings.

White-winged scoters nest in a wide variety of locations, including forested lakes, prairie potholes, and the arctic tundra. In winter they concentrate in saltwater bays. At that season, their food consists mostly of mussels and other shellfish; they seem to feed most commonly at depths of fifteen to twenty feet.

Nesting birds of this species have the curious habit of covering their eggs with loose soil as the clutch accumulates. Once all the eggs are laid, down is used instead, as with other ducks. In the meantime, looking for scoter eggs has been described (by Herbert K. Job) as "like digging potatoes."

Length 19-23½ inches. Female, Swan Lake, British Columbia, November.

7

Hooded Merganser

LOPHODYTES CUCULLATUS

plate 7

Hooded Merganser - LOPHODYTES CUCULLATUS

THE merganser or "fish duck" tribe has come up with the most extreme specialization in the duck family. In the small hooded merganser it has produced what some consider one of the world's loveliest waterfowl. The little drake is able to fan his black-tipped white crest forward to a fully erect position and habitually does so. This flashing white "heliograph" is one way to recognize him at a distance.

The peculiar bill of a merganser is unique among waterfowl. Instead of the broad, spatulate bill of other ducks, evolution has provided just the instrument for catching and hanging onto slippery fish. Long, narrow, and with backward-directed "teeth" in both mandibles, the merganser's bill is a classic example of extreme adaptation to a very specialized line of work. Of course no bird has true teeth. The sharp points are fine but sturdy serrations in the bill itself.

The hooded merganser is another of the tree-nesting ducks. It looks for streams and ponds that are well wooded right to the edge. Occasionally it will use a stump standing in the water, and, rarely, it may come to a bird box.

Look for this bird in flooded forests with open patches of water. But you may look in vain; the beautiful hooded merganser is no longer common. North America underwent and is still enduring the last paroxysms of a widespread trophy-shooting dementia, manifest still in uncountable hooded mergansers picking up dust on mantelpieces and gathering cobwebs on boathouse ledges throughout the vacation country. This is a most unwary species – too tame for its own good. Any dolt can kill one.

As you would expect, the hooded merganser is an expert swimmer and diver. It can make its living in rather fast water, unlike most other diving ducks. Small pond fish are its normal fare – rarely or never those of any commercial value.

Length 16-19 inches. Male, Seven Oaks, Florida, December.
Female, Lake Scugog, Ontario, October.

8

Red-breasted Merganser

MERGUS SERRATOR

Red-breasted Merganser - MERGUS SERRATOR

ANY bird that eats fish is faced, sooner or later, with the problem that is common to all animals that eat anything that man also eats. Mergansers eat fish; *ergo* mergansers are bad. If, like so many other ducks, they ate pondweed (man cannot digest pondweed), mergansers would be good. They would also be good to eat. But they are not at all good to eat, and this, plus their diet, weights the balance against them. Mergansers are often described by some gunners and fishermen as "worthless" or "undesirable."

It is true that these birds occasionally eat fish when and where they should not; usually this is a very local event. A merganser in a fish hatchery must be discouraged immediately. So must an intruding mink, but a mink is anything but worthless. The isolated malfeasance of one individual should never be allowed to develop into a blanket indictment of a species as a whole. In fact, most mergansers (like all other predators) take the line of least resistance; they use the prey species most readily available and most easily caught. Slow-moving coarse fish are much easier to catch than fast and agile game fish, and they are much more abundant in the waters occupied by this species. The odds favour the taking of coarse fish, which, not surprisingly, is exactly what happens.

The red-breasted merganser is somewhat more gregarious than other species and even acts co-operatively upon occasion. A string of birds will take position in line abreast and drive a school of fish into shallow water where it is easier to catch them. Whether this is an abstract relating of cause and effect or only an "instinctive" pattern of behaviour is open to question.

This species always nests on the ground, usually on the shore of a spruce-rimmed lake. Eight to ten buffy-olive eggs are laid in a downy depression, usually beneath a sheltering bush or small tree. In the late autumn, after the breeding season, enormous flocks of these birds may be seen in migration on the southern Great Lakes, streaming toward the coast and their winter fishing grounds on salt water in the southern states.

Length 19½-26 inches. Female, Departure Bay, British Columbia, March.
Male, Long Point, Ontario, November.

9

Goshawk

ACCIPITER GENTILIS

Goshawk - ACCIPITER GENTILIS

As the very model of killing efficiency, the goshawk has few peers in the world of birds of prey. From its blood-red eye to its chilling talons, this majestic creature is the end product of an evolutionary process that took millions upon millions of years. The result is the last word in bird control. It is a fact of life that all animals – including songbirds – must have population controls. Some people who claim to love birds are horrified by the activities of hawks, but it must be remembered that hawks are part of nature's system. They can do nothing else; hawks are committed to the existence to which they have become adapted.

The goshawk is an *accipiter,* a true hawk. Other birds that we informally call "hawks," such as the falcons, the soaring buteos, and the harriers, all have their distinctive characteristics, and they are not hawks. The true hawks have short, rounded wings and long tails. They are low and stealthy fliers, hedge-hopping toward the unsuspecting target, and show marvelous manoeuvrability in wooded areas, dodging between branches, beneath shrubs, and around thickets with astonishing speed and accuracy for good-sized birds. In unhurried flight, the usual procedure is to take several flaps, sail for a distance, and then flap again. There are three true hawks in Canada; the goshawk, which is larger than a crow, is the greatest.

This fine predator is widespread, but not common. The abundance of birds of prey depends upon the numbers of their prey. Contrary to popular belief, a predator does not usually have any appreciable effect upon the numbers of the animals it eats. For example, a given patch of forest has room in it for only so many flickers. Flickers sometimes lay ten or a dozen eggs. Surplus flickers have to be eliminated one way or another. To be dispatched instantly by a goshawk, as the flicker in the plate was, would seem a kinder fate than some of the alternatives, which include starvation or disease. The very fact that we are not "up to here in flickers" attests to the presence of the goshawk, together with a long list of other predators, parasites, and miscellaneous controlling agents.

This is a fast, agile, and powerful bird, capable of killing prey the size of a pheasant or rabbit. It is much admired by falconers, not only for its efficiency, but also for its legendary ferocity. It is willing to hunt all day, where other species might tire or lose interest after one or two kills.

Length 20-26 inches. Wingspread 3½-4 feet. Male, Boyle, Alberta, November.

10

Osprey

PANDION HALIAETUS

Osprey - PANDION HALIAETUS

THE "fish hawk" is found in greater or lesser numbers over a considerable part of the world. Almost as large as an eagle (larger than some), and strikingly marked, this glorious bird is beautifully adapted to its specialty – fishing. It has a strong, hooked beak, the ability to hover in mid-air almost motionless, acute eyesight, and the most unusual feet of any bird of prey. The talons are especially long and curved, and the toes themselves are equipped with short, sharp spines to help the bird grasp and hold its slippery prey.

The osprey hunts by quartering a lake or bay, always on the lookout for fish basking near the surface. Spotting one, it plummets down in a more or less steep dive and hits the water feet first with a spectacular splash. The bird may actually disappear for an instant. As it rises from the water, it usually manages to hold the fish head first, to cut down on air resistance. It then laboriously climbs to cruising altitude and flaps away toward a huge nest of sticks high in the top of an isolated tree.

The osprey's exclusive dependence on fish may be its undoing. Not that there is any shortage of fish; the coarse species that make up the bulk of its diet are in good supply. Unfortunately, the osprey is one of the more frequent victims of the most terrible biotic scourge of all time – the chain-reaction effect of chemical pesticides in our living environment.

Fish and other cold-blooded animals have a low metabolic rate. They are able to build up in their systems substantial quantities of toxic chemicals picked up in their food, but not necessarily enough to kill them. These chemicals are pesticides that are washed from the forests and agricultural lands into our water systems. The fish then pass on a concentrated dose of the poison to the higher, warm-blooded animal that may eat *them*, and whose tolerance may be considerably less. It has been found in recent years that ospreys in areas of high pesticide contamination (river mouths and estuaries) are no longer breeding successfully. Their infertile eggs contain high levels of DDT, its derivatives, and related substances.

Ospreys have dropped alarmingly in numbers. It is quite possible that the age of technology will have claimed this irreplaceable species before many more years have passed.

Length 21-24½ inches. Wingspread 4½-6 feet. Female, Coldstream, Ontario, April.

11

Peregrine Falcon

FALCO PEREGRINUS

plate 11

Peregrine Falcon - FALCO PEREGRINUS

THE breath-taking aerial performance of the prince of falcons has excited and elated the heart and mind of man for a thousand years. No spectacle in the bird world can surpass the shattering stoop of the peregrine, which has been variously estimated at from 90 to 175 m.p.h. Woe betide the selected duck or pigeon, however swift, struck in mid-flight by a terrible missile that came without warning from out of the depths of the wide blue sky.

The sky is the peregrine's element, the cliff face its home. There are larger falcons, but few are swifter, and, certainly, none is more renowned. This species is the next thing to cosmopolitan. There are a variety of forms; the peregrine of the Queen Charlotte Islands and coastal Alaska, for example, is much darker than the one pictured here.

The peregrine is big-headed, bullet-shaped, and pointed-winged; it is built for whistling speed and crunching impact. No wonder it is the toast of falconers, who are willing to fly lesser species if necessary, but who know no substitute for the genuine article. Falconry is not widely practised in Canada, but there are pockets of it. It is to be hoped that the enthusiasm of the falconers does not have an adverse effect upon the numbers of the falcons. The peregrine can probably no longer withstand nest-robbing for the purposes of falconry, as it is already in grievous trouble from another direction.

Like the osprey, the peregrine stands at the apex of a food "pyramid"; it eats animals which eat lesser animals which eat plants. In many parts of our continent, this food chain is inoculated with deadly poisons which rise through each level to the bird of prey at the top. In the last five to ten years, the peregrine has disappeared as a breeding bird in the eastern United States. The same thing is happening in Britain. Though there is insufficient information on Canadian peregrines, the story would seem to be the same. Chemical pesticides are responsible. Their eventual effects on the whole inter-related wildlife community, in the light of developments with the birds of prey, can only be guessed at.

Length 15-21 inches. Wingspread 3¼-3¾ feet. Male, Vernon, British Columbia, October.

12

Pigeon Hawk

FALCO COLUMBARIUS

Pigeon Hawk - FALCO COLUMBARIUS

DESPITE its name, the pigeon "hawk" is not a hawk at all, but a small, jay-sized falcon something like a scaled-down peregrine. Its name derives not from the fact that it eats pigeons (it doesn't), but that it looks superficially like a pigeon when in flight. It has the typical pointed wings, longish tail, and rapid, powerful flight of the falcons.

A much better vernacular name for this species is "merlin." It goes by that name in Britain, as it has for hundreds of years – ever since the golden days of mediaeval falconry, when the small merlins were considered appropriate for ladies to fly. Peregrines and the giant gyrfalcon were reserved for top-level males in the complex and iron-clad hierarchy of the sport.

The merlin is found throughout the higher latitudes of the northern hemisphere, breeding as far up as the limit of trees. Though it sticks to the spruce-fir environment for nesting, it is not at all fussy about precise sites. Old magpies' and crows' nests are sometimes used, and even hollows in the ground and the disused excavations of woodpeckers in dead trees. Like the peregrine, this species is quite variable in colour, and again like the peregrine, the form on the Pacific coast is very dark, almost black.

This is a small bird, but a fearless one. It commonly badgers, hounds, and chivvies much larger birds, including crows and great horned owls. Its prey is much more modest; sparrow-sized small birds and large insects account for most of its diet. Among the latter, dragonflies are especially important, plus grasshoppers butterflies, and others. The merlin sometimes feeds, kite-like, on the wing. It likes to maintain a lookout on a bare twig or high rock from which it can survey the food possibilities, darting after its prey in typical falcon style. It may be the only bird capable of catching swallows on the wing.

The handsome little merlin is not common anywhere, but may be seen most readily during migration, when it often accompanies flocks of longspurs, various sandpipers, and others. Thus it has a food supply for the entire journey.

Length 10-13½ inches. Wingspread 2 feet.

13

Spruce Grouse

CANACHITES CANADENSIS

Spruce Grouse - CANACHITES CANADENSIS

THE stiff and ritualized courtship ceremony of the spruce grouse is one of the most magnificent sights of the deep evergreen woods. The strutting, posturing male seems on the verge of exploding as he erects his plumage to the fullest extent and advertises himself unceasingly on his own private parade ground. The drab-coloured hen, seemingly nonchalant about it all, will eventually react appropriately.

This sequestered mating of a woodland species is in contrast with the orgiastic social performances of such open country species as the sharp-tailed and sage grouse and the prairie chicken, all of which indulge in mass courtship and at least some promiscuity. The remote and shaded retreat of the spruce grouse is the perfect backdrop for the male's resplendent plumage.

For all its striking appearance, however, the spruce grouse is remarkably camouflaged. Its apparent blind faith in this method of concealment has earned it the wretched nickname "fool hen." When the bird is disturbed on the forest floor, it promptly flies up into the nearest tree, becomes perfectly still, and lets its protective colouration take over from there. This does not always work, however, and many a starving woodsman has taken advantage of this to knock the bird over with a stick, only to use the ungrateful adjective "stupid" for the bird's providential co-operation.

But the spruce grouse is edible only in an emergency. Its diet consists chiefly of spruce needles and the buds of these and other conifers, which, apparently, is more than evident in its flesh. In summer, it may turn to berries and other such fare, while the young, like those of most birds, stick in the early stages to animal protein in the form of insects and other invertebrates.

This is a sedentary bird; it rarely moves far from its home base, and it is non-migratory. That is a boon to birdwatchers, for prior knowledge of traditional spruce grouse locations saves a great deal of searching for a surprisingly inconspicuous bird.

Length 15-17 inches. Female, Parry Sound, Ontario, October.
Male, St. Fabien de Panet, Quebec, October.

14

Common Snipe

CAPELLA GALLINAGO

Common Snipe - CAPELLA GALLINAGO

THIS unusual sandpiper is found in appropriate locations throughout the northern part of the northern hemisphere. Its chosen haunts are variable, but there is a common denominator – water. It nests at the borders of marshes and wet bogs. In migration it turns up in roadside ditches, in soggy fields, and wherever there is enough water and damp grassy cover to accommodate it.

Like the related woodcock, the snipe has a heavy-set, stocky body, short legs, relatively large eyes set far back on the head, and a truly enormous bill. The size of the bill is by no means its only peculiarity. It is essentially a probing instrument, for reaching deep into mud and soft soil for worms. Like some item of the most refined surgical hardware, it has a flexible tip for seeking and seizing its evasive target.

Even more remarkable is the snipe's bizarre specialization for purposes of courtship. At night (or by day if it is overcast), the bird flies up to a considerable height, then hurtles earthward emitting a strange, hollow, "winnowing" sound which ceases as it swings aloft again. For many years, the source of this singular humming vibration was unknown; argument surrounded it until relatively recently. It is now known that it is not a vocal note, but an instrumental or mechanical one produced by the tail.

The snipe's tail is specially adapted for the purpose. When it is fanned, its two stiff outer feathers are separated from the rest and vibrate in the air as the bird shoots downward. At the same time, the wings are stiffly agitated and have the effect of allowing air to strike the tail at regular (rapid) intervals. The result is the tremulous *vibrato* music so characteristic of cold bogs in the June darkness.

The snipe does not limit itself to mechanical sound. It has a song of sorts which can often be heard in between "winnows." Not content with aerobatics, the bird also struts like a little turkey on the ground.

Length 10½-11½ inches. Male, Puntchesakut Lake, British Columbia, May.

15

Solitary Sandpiper

TRINGA SOLITARIA

Solitary Sandpiper - TRINGA SOLITARIA

THE overwhelming majority of sandpipers frequent marshes, lakeshores, and other flat, open, water margins. As befits their habitat, they nest on the ground. The attractive solitary sandpiper does neither of these things. It has forsaken the traditional haunts and habits of sandpipers in favour of the unusual environment of the northern forest; it has defied convention by nesting in trees.

The vast evergreen country of the north abounds in tiny wooded ponds, streams, and forested bogs. This is the retreat of the solitary sandpiper. Like its kind, it is never far from water, but it is satisfied with a very modest supply. It chooses a cool wet swamp more or less heavily overgrown with spruces and tamaracks, and there it seeks out the old, last year's nests of tree-dwelling species such as robins, rusty blackbirds, jays, waxwings, and others. Then, like its close relative of the Old World, the green sandpiper, it proceeds to make the old nest its own. This may be in a tree from four to forty feet high, a most improbable site for a true sandpiper.

Young sandpipers are precocial. They are born fully able to get about by themselves, like young ducks, geese, loons, and many more. Since they must feed themselves, they begin to forage immediately. Presumably the four young solitary sandpipers vacate the nest in much the same way as young goldeneyes are thought to do: they merely fall as gracefully as possible to a soft, sphagnum-cushioned carpet, and under the parent's watchful eye set about making a living.

Food consists of all forms of aquatic animal life, including insects, small crustaceans, and many others which it will stir from the muddy bottom of shallow water with its feet. Occasionally the bird will take an insect on the wing, snapping it up as a flycatcher would. There is no shortage of food in the muskeg. This is a good thing, as solitary sandpipers need plenty of fuel in the form of fat for their autumn migration southward. They winter as far from the spruce country as the West Indies, southern Mexico, and Argentina.

Length 7½-9 inches. Female, Favourable Lake, Ontario, July.

16

Lesser Yellowlegs

TOTANUS FLAVIPES

Lesser Yellowlegs - TOTANUS FLAVIPES

THERE are two species of yellowlegs – the lesser and the greater. The two are distressingly similar in appearance, so much so that it is frequently difficult to distinguish them unless they happen to be together for comparison. But there are differences. This species is much smaller than the other. Its bill is quite straight; that of the greater is perceptibly upturned. Most important, their call notes are distinctive.

This species breeds in open evergreen forests from Alaska to northern Ontario and Quebec. Unlike the tree-nesting solitary sandpiper, which likes the relatively dense thickets around spruce bogs, the yellowlegs prefers muskeg country with more sparse tree cover. Appropriately for a sandpiper, it nests in a hollow on the ground.

Its liking for rather open woods suggests that the lesser yellowlegs might be one of those species which can benefit from forest fire. A mature, dense forest is unsuitable for it; clearings with a pioneer growth of post-fire poplar or aspen saplings are more to its taste.

It is a paradox that some species *must* have at least occasional fire for their very existence. One of these is Kirtland's warbler, which nests only in jack pine of a certain age (and size) in Michigan. Jack pine must have the intense heat of fire for the release of seeds from its cones, so this rare warbler is inextricably bound to conflagration for its survival. The same may be true, to a lesser extent, of the yellowlegs.

Both yellowlegs have loud, shrill cries, and they are very vocal around the nest. Most shorebirds call a great deal of attention to themselves when they have eggs and young, the effect of which is to distract the attention of predators from the brood. Yellowlegs display themselves conspicuously and become exceptionally noisy when an intruder comes anywhere near the nesting site.

All our shorebirds are good fliers, and most are long-distance migrants, moving between forty and fifty miles per hour for remarkable distances. One lesser yellowlegs, banded on Cape Cod, was recovered six days later in Martinique, nineteen hundred miles away – an average of three hundred and sixteen miles per day. This species winters as far south as Chile and Argentina.

Length 9½-11 inches. Male, Fort Severn, Ontario, June.

17

Great Horned Owl

BUBO VIRGINIANUS

Great Horned Owl - BUBO VIRGINIANUS

It is likely that no North American bird has aroused such extremes of human admiration and antipathy as this great owl. Those who know something about the bird hold it in unassailable esteem; many of those who do not are its most implacable enemies. As in all extremes of opinion, the truth lies somewhere in between, although as biological literacy makes slow and laboriously-won inroads among our prejudices, it becomes increasingly difficult – in fact impossible – to condemn any wildlife species.

This is our most powerful and aggressive owl. It will eat any animal it can overcome, and the list of its victims is long. Its menu runs from voles and mice to rabbits, skunks, and even house cats, from insects and small birds to pheasants and grouse. This is what gets the horned owl into trouble. When it eats some item that is equally or even more desirable to man (usually for the purpose of sport killing), loud and strong are the brays of recrimination.

Most predators are lazy. They take the food most readily available, and the prey most easily caught is clearly the species that happens to be most abundant at the time. Populations of grouse, for example, are cyclic; they have dramatic swings through peaks and hollows of abundance on a fairly predictable schedule. In years of grouse "explosions," horned owls take a lot of grouse. In years of vole abundance, owls will depend on them for the bulk of their food. Neither makes any real difference, because the predator depends for its living on the numbers of its prey, and has little if any influence on those numbers. Neither (except in cases of excessive killing, such as that of prairie waterfowl) does the hunter. Both normally take only a portion of natural annual surpluses that one way or another have to be trimmed anyway for the benefit of the wildlife community as a whole.

Yet this excellent bird is persecuted viciously and is legally unprotected in parts of the continent where the traditional pioneer attitudes towards wildlife still prevail. Happily it has no significant enemies save man, and is able to maintain its numbers reasonably well in those wilderness areas where it is undisturbed.

The horned owl breeds very early in the year, usually in the old nest of a crow or hawk, sometimes in a hollow tree. It is not at all rare to see the old bird incubating her eggs with snow lying on her back and all around her. This is our most formidable bird in defence of its nest, and is not content with threats, as most species are. Many a bird bander can testify that climbing to a horned owl's nest is a calculated risk. The bird does not know fear, and is savagely armed to deal with interlopers.

Length 20-25 inches. Female, Algoma District, Ontario, February.

18

Hawk-Owl

SURNIA ULULA

Hawk-Owl - SURNIA ULULA

Few birds are more appropriately named than this one; although a proper owl in all vital respects, its long tail and hunting technique are distinctly hawk-like. This is a good example of the process called evolutionary convergence. When owls came into being and began to proliferate over the world, there was clearly no need for all of them to be strictly nocturnal. There were possibilities for at least some owls to become crepuscular, or even diurnal. There was an ecological opportunity to be exploited by an owl that would hunt by day, more or less in the style of a hawk. That, evidently, is what happened. An owl found a new niche and occupied it. In the process of becoming adapted to this sort of life, it came to resemble a hawk somewhat, but the two families are not related.

This is an owl of the far north where the summer nights are short. At the season when young must be fed, there is more daylight than darkness to hunt by, so it benefits the bird to work in the daytime, like the snowy owl of even farther north. Just as a merlin or kestrel would, the hawk-owl perches on a tall prominent spike or other vantage point, reviewing the surrounding muskeg. When a small mammal is spotted, the owl launches itself in pursuit. It has everything going for it: the silent, buoyant flight of the owl, the speed of the hawk. It is a singularly efficient, though nowhere common, predator on mice and voles. Probably there are sufficient hawks in the same general line of business to keep the competition healthy.

As you might expect, the hawk-owl's nesting routine is not unlike that of one of the small hawks. It generally nests in a cavity in a tree (often one made by a pileated woodpecker), but it will also use the abandoned nest of a crow or hawk, like many other owls.

Owls can see perfectly well in the daytime. Light blindness is a myth, although some species may see better than others in daylight. The owl's peculiarity is that it can see remarkably well in *minimum* light; its eyes are especially adapted to allow it to take advantage of the slightest illumination. In total darkness, however, with no light source at all, an owl can see no better than any other animal, including man.

Length 14½-17½ inches. Male, Big Hay Lake, Alberta, October.

Great Gray Owl - STRIX NEBULOSA

WITH its great puffy head, yellow eyes, and the concentric, "op art" circles of its facial discs, this northern owl is the most striking of them all. It is also the largest over all, because of its unusually long tail, but its size is mostly illusion. Although its measurements are greater than those of either the snowy or great horned owls, the great gray is mostly fluff. It is heavily and thickly feathered, and the body within is quite slight. It weighs considerably less than either of its sturdy relatives.

Since it is not as strong and fearsome as its size would suggest, this species concentrates on smaller food sources than the horned owl. Mice, voles, chipmunks, and other small mammals predominate; it is probably not a serious threat to most birds. Thus its food habits are almost entirely "beneficial," to use an archaism that is happily disappearing from natural history literature. It used to be conventional to categorize wildlife species in this way, but no animal, obviously, is either "harmful" or "beneficial," except in the most subjective human terms, and these are terms that do not apply in nature.

Man does a great deal of rationalizing in his attitudes towards other animals. It is all right to shoot hawks and owls because these birds are "killers." Of course they are killers. That is what they are designed to do; that is their service to the natural system. No other animal has human concepts or human motives; nature knows neither evil nor good. In the complex chain of nature, all living things play their part. No link in that chain is "bad"; each link has its function.

The great gray owl is notably tame. On those rare occasions when one or two individuals turn up during the winter in some settled part of the country, they are nearly always – but not always – approachable and unwary. This has led to an inevitable thinning of great gray owl numbers wherever it has regularly come into contact with man. Luckily for the bird, it is a wilderness species and does not commonly encounter its only enemy.

Length 24-33 inches. Male, Winnipeg, Manitoba, January.

19

Great Gray Owl

STRIX NEBULOSA

20

Long-eared Owl

ASIO OTUS

Long-eared Owl - ASIO OTUS

DESPITE its appearance and its name, the ears of this owl are well concealed beneath its feathers and are no longer than those of any other owl. The conspicuous "ears" on the head are only tufts of feathers. Like the "horns" of the great horned owl, they are merely adornments.

This does not mean that owls' ears are not remarkable. They are quite unlike those of any other birds. The ears of some owls have unusually large openings in the sides of the head, to which are fitted flaps that can be raised at will. They work like a cupped hand in reflecting sound waves toward the very large eardrum. Owls are extraordinarily sensitive to high-frequency sounds like the squeak of a mouse and to sounds of very low intensity such as the footfall of a rabbit. In some species the ears are asymmetrical, pointing in different directions, and this is thought to aid the bird in sound location. Since owls can see no better in complete darkness than any other animals can, their ears are of the greatest importance on heavily overcast nights. In experimental situations, in the total absence of light, owls have zeroed in on their prey with astonishing accuracy, by hearing alone.

The eyes of most birds are placed on the sides of the head, so that they have only limited vision to the front. That is why a chicken or a robin cocks its head in the familiar way. But if a bird is going to specialize in catching quick-moving prey, it needs stereoscopic vision in order to be able to judge distances accurately. Placement of the eyes in front, with overlapping binocular vision in an arc up to 70°, makes the owl's pounce precise.

Unlike the eyes of mammals, birds' eyes are fixed in their sockets. They cannot move around. If a bird cannot move its eyes, it must move its head. Owls have developed amazing efficiency in this respect. An otherwise motionless long-eared owl can swivel its head through a full 270° before it must unscrew its neck and go round the other way.

Length 13-16 inches. Female, Simcoe, Ontario, November.

21

Boreal Owl

AEGOLIUS FUNEREUS

plate 21

Boreal Owl - AEGOLIUS FUNEREUS

TENGMALM'S owl is the Old World name for this northern species which is also known on this continent as Richardson's owl. But it is the same bird – a small, chunky owl of the coniferous forest that is not commonly seen in settled parts of the country.

Since most owls hunt at night or at twilight, they have little to do during the daytime except to digest the meal of the night before. Owls swallow their prey whole or in gullet-sized chunks. Indigestible portions such as skulls, bones, feathers and fur are regurgitated in the form of tightly packed pellets that look as though they were made of felt. (In a sense, they are.) During this digestive process the bird prefers to remain well hidden. Most owls choose a dense concealing evergreen in which to roost, and they usually stay as close to the trunk as possible.

The cryptic camouflage of owls is so excellent that they easily go unnoticed. Both this species and the closely related and even smaller saw-whet owl will sit so tightly and remain so still, relying on their protective colouration, that they can be touched and even caught by hand. This tameness is often their undoing when they are spotted by the wrong party, for the ignorant are still very much with us. Hawk and owl persecution is by no means a thing of the past.

As with other owls (and hawks) the female is the larger of the sexes. This bird nests in a cavity in a tree – usually an old woodpecker dig. An interesting courtship rite has been observed, in the course of which the birds indulge in symbolic feeding. The male does much calling while flying back and forth at the selected nesting hole. When the female is at last induced to enter the chamber, there she finds a delectable fresh mouse. Presumably this is difficult to resist.

The boreal owl is a particularly effective hunter, concentrating on small nocturnal mammals. For this kind of life, extraordinary hearing and eyesight are not the only advantages enjoyed by owls. They have very large wings in relation to their weight, which enables them to fly unusually slowly, with a low flapping rate and a very low stalling speed. This allows them great manoeuvrability. Their downy, soft feathers are virtually soundless; the owl's approach and strike are silent and sure.

Length 8½-12 inches. Male, Port Credit, Ontario, March.

22

Black-backed Three-toed Woodpecker

PICOIDES ARCTICUS

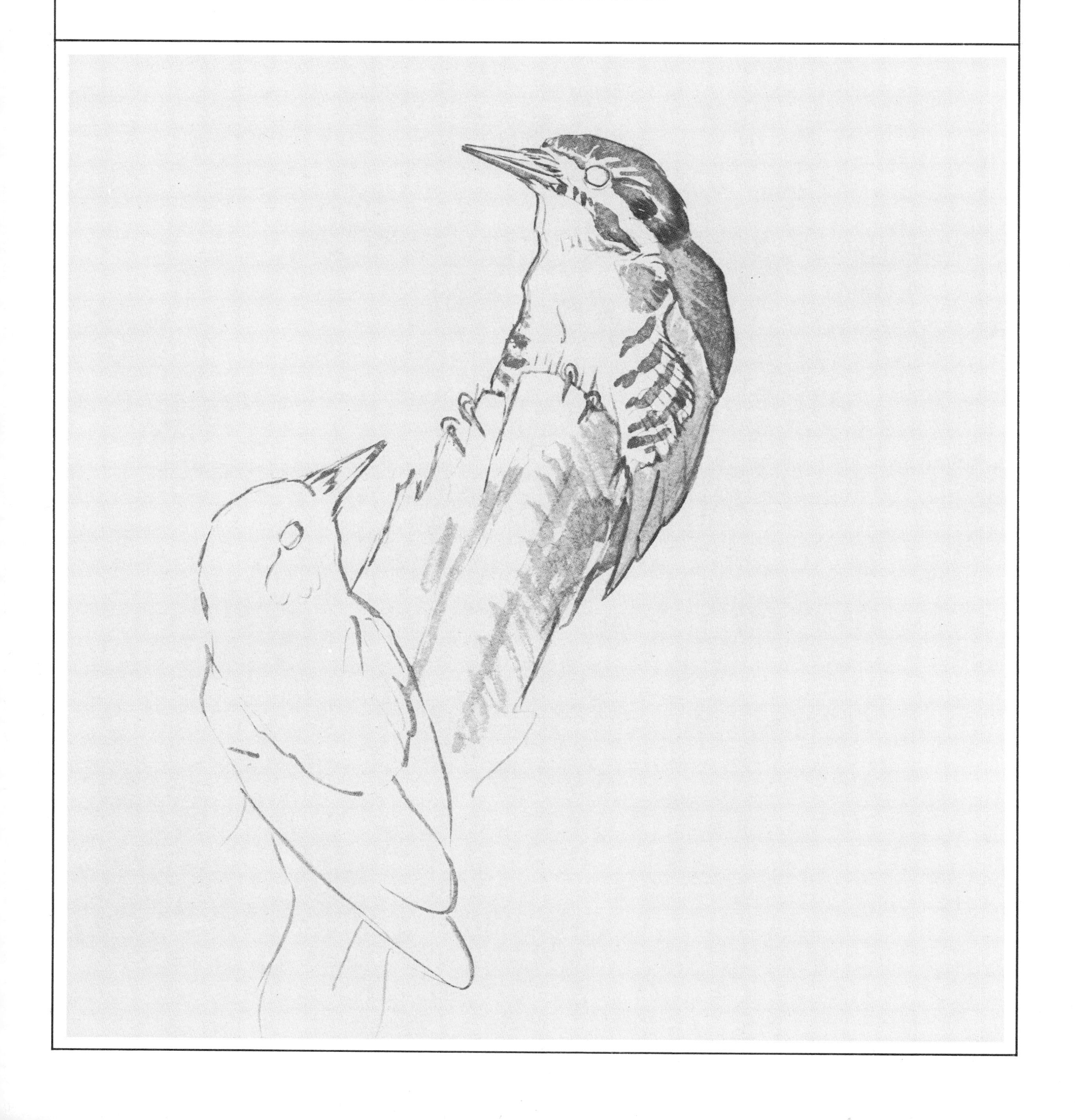

Black-backed Three-toed Woodpecker - PICOIDES ARCTICUS

The specific name *arcticus* of this handsome woodpecker is somewhat misleading. The true arctic, a treeless desert, is clearly no place for a woodpecker. In fact this is the more southern in distribution of the two members of this genus, though both are birds of the northern forest of spruce, larch, and fir.

That it has only three toes instead of the normal complement of four does not seem to impair the efficiency of what is otherwise a perfectly typical member of its family. Woodpeckers' feet are stronger than those of many birds, enabling them to feed hour after hour in a near-vertical position, clinging to the bark. One toe more or less does not seem to make much difference. Why one should have been lost in the course of evolution is unclear, though it has been suggested that the elimination of one toe may in some way be an aid to greater pecking force.

In recent years this species has become increasingly familiar to the army of birdwatchers in the southern parts of Canada. At one time the sight of a three-toed woodpecker of either species was a source of great excitement and much agitated communication along the birders' hot lines. This is no longer so in many regions, especially in southern Ontario. Each winter substantial numbers of this species are seen as far south as Lake Ontario – and in the USA, a good distance beyond.

Sporadic, irregular southward movement in some winters is characteristic of several northern birds, including some of the owls, but the appearance of this woodpecker has become an annual event. No one knows what causes the birds to forsake the spruce belt, but there is some evidence to indicate that once in the south, they are kept there for the winter by an abundance of food.

This annual woodpecker bonanza is apparently the result of the widespread ravages of imported Dutch elm disease. Southern Ontario, for example, is now littered with dead and dying elms, and a great many of these trees show conspicuous patches where the bark has been flaked away. This is the normal feeding pattern of this species. The bark layers of dead trees are filled with the larvae of bark-boring beetles and other insects upon which these birds depend for food. Most woodpeckers do not customarily dig in healthy trees; their prey can only occur normally in *un*healthy or dead ones.

Length 9-10 inches. Male, Favourable Lake, Ontario, October.
Female, Lac la Nonne, Alberta, September.

23

Northern Three-toed Woodpecker

PICOIDES TRIDACTYLUS

Northern Three-toed Woodpecker - PICOIDES TRIDACTYLUS

LIKE the preceding species, this woodpecker has strong feet for clutching bark, regardless of the number of toes. It has the typical chisel-like bill of a woodpecker, mounted on a large, heavy skull and driven by a strong and flexible neck. The tongues of woodpeckers are especially designed to penetrate deeply into dead wood. They can be extended for an astonishing length, and carry various types of barbs and bristles for impaling and dragging out their prey. A nice accessory bit of equipment consists of special bristle-like feathers covering the nostrils and protecting them from tiny chips and "saw dust." A woodpecker's tail is notably stiff in order to prop the bird firmly and securely against tree trunks.

Unlike the black-backed three-toed woodpecker, which is confined to North America, this species occurs in Eurasia as well. It is rather more northern in distribution than the other and appears to be much less common. Both depend for their livelihood on the natural mortality of northern evergreens due to such agents as disease, fire, and flooding, all of which occur more or less regularly.

We are too often inclined to think of such tree-killing events as "disasters," and to forget that they have always been a part of the natural process. Without a continuing kill of trees there could be no woodpeckers. Just as fire promotes the spread of white-tailed deer, for example, by providing luxuriant, mixed second growth, it also supplies dead trees and a new larder of wood-boring insects for the woodpeckers. Just as the beaver, by flooding the landscape, improves the habitat for water-loving moose, it also makes drowned trees available to the woodpeckers' insect prey. Rarely does anything happen in nature that fails to bring someone some good. Even the infamous spruce budworm, by thinning the balsam fir forest, promotes a new natural succession of events of benefit to many plant and animal species and of significance to the life cycle of the forest itself.

All woodpeckers excavate their nesting sites in dead wood. They do not line their nests; the chips are let fall where they may, including the bottom of the cavity where the white eggs are deposited. Both sexes take part in the duties associated with nesting. They appear to look after the young for an unusually long period after they have taken to the wing. Perhaps young woodpeckers must take extra time to develop adequate strength in bill, head and neck before they can begin to do their own digging.

Length 8-9½ inches. Female, Savanne, Ontario, July.
Male, Kenora District, Ontario, June.

24

Yellow-bellied Flycatcher

EMPIDONAX FLAVIVENTRIS

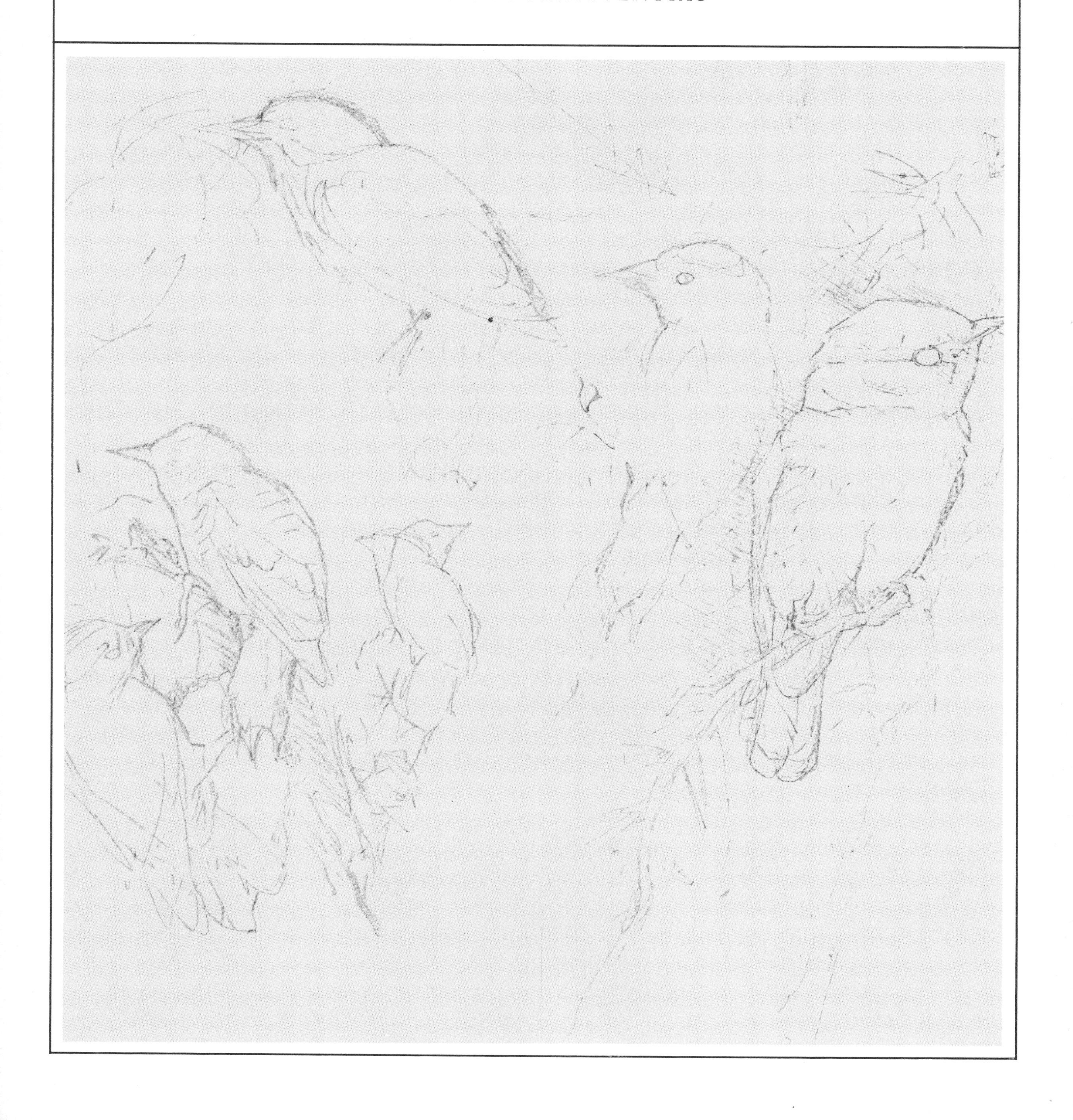

Yellow-bellied Flycatcher - EMPIDONAX FLAVIVENTRIS

SHY and inconspicuous for a flycatcher, this delicate little species nests in the evergreen forest east of the Rockies. It is one of the bewildering members of the genus *Empidonax*, seven of which occur in Canada (there are two more in the USA), all of which look so much alike that they have long been the despair of both expert field students and (especially) beginners. This one, luckily, is usually identifiable by its yellow underparts and by its yellow throat, which is marked strongly enough to make identification reasonably safe, even though some of its relatives appear somewhat yellowish in the fall.

The more experienced a bird student becomes, the less inclined he is to attempt to separate the *Empidonax* flycatchers in the field, except on the basis of voice; the songs and call notes of the various species are distinctive. This one is so retiring that often its call is the only clue to its presence, although in common with other flycatchers, it can scarcely be called a "singer." Flycatchers' voices are usually harsh and discordant.

This is the only member of its genus that habitually nests on the ground, in a cup-like structure deep in the soft mossy floor of the spruce-muskeg country, so artfully concealed that it is rarely found. There are said to be two cups, or sections, one fitting into the other. The inner cup is described as being well insulated from the constant dampness of the sphagnum bog.

Typically, flycatchers have broad, rather flat bills, surrounded by long bristles which help to trap their prey. Since it regularly takes flying insects on the wing, a flycatcher need not be so much a fast flier as a strong and manoeuvrable one. Its aerial acrobatics in pursuit of winged insects are extremely interesting. At one time it was thought that hummingbirds were the only birds actually capable of flying backward. Flycatchers have been observed to do something very *like* flying backward; certainly they are able to hover in one position, at the same time achieving a variety of subtle movements in apparently any direction.

Length 5-5¾ inches. Male, Hamilton, Ontario, May.

25

Olive-sided Flycatcher

NUTTALLORNIS BOREALIS

Olive-sided Flycatcher - NUTTALLORNIS BOREALIS

Many flycatchers are strident, vociferous, aggressive birds, and this species is as noisily belligerent as any. It is so competitive about its nesting territory that although it is a common species, it is rather widely scattered through the boreal forest country. Olive-sided flycatchers do not like excessive proximity to their own species, and indeed will frequently drive off other birds as well.

This is an easily identifiable, middle-sized, very sturdy flycatcher with a big head and a drab olive "waistcoat." It likes to station itself bolt upright on the very topmost spire of a spruce or some other evergreen, maintaining a constant watch for passing bees, flies, and winged ants, and watching too for other birds to drive away. When not actually on the wing, it remains quite motionless and would easily go undetected, were it not for its unmistakeable "song," which has been variously expressed from "Hip – three cheers!" to "Hic – three beers!" The verbalization of bird song is a woefully unsatisfactory means of description, as a song can be interpreted differently by every human listener, but in this case at least, the rhythm and phrasing are constant.

Its preferred habitat usually includes water – spruce bogs and muskeg, small forest lakes, streams, and ponds. The nest itself is nearly always in a conifer, often on one of the lower horizontal branches. Incubation of the three eggs takes almost exactly two weeks, and the young are reported to remain in the nest for about three weeks more.

Flycatchers are forced to be migrants; their food demands it. This one winters in Central America and the northwestern part of South America. In the spring, the northward movement of flycatchers must coincide with hatches of flying insects, and thus it is tied to the temperature. This makes the birds vulnerable to sudden drops of the thermometer, and if a cold spell develops during their flight in May, sometimes they are forced to seek insects and other invertebrates on the ground, or even to turn to vegetable food for a meal or two until things improve. However, since this species is so attracted to bees, and some bees often venture forth in surprisingly cool weather, its food supply is reasonably dependable.

Length 7-8 inches. Male, Algoma District, Ontario, June.

Gray Jay - PERISOREUS CANADENSIS

NOTWITHSTANDING the shocked protests of diehard chauvinists and those of us too old to become unstuck from the nomenclature of our childhood, the Canada jay officially became the gray jay with the 1957 publication of the fifth edition of the American Ornithologists' Union *Check-list of North American Birds.* Actually it was a very good idea, as we already had the blue jay and the green jay. Since this bird breeds in evergreen forests as far south as California, the parochial name really did not suit. Old-timers will continue to call the bird "whiskey-jack" anyway.

This must be one of the most familiar birds of the north country, yet the dark young bird always seems to cause confusion. An adult gray jay looks something like an over-insulated giant chickadee, and is immediately identifiable, but in the immature plumage it looks like a different bird.

No camper in the spruce forest or the western mountains can fail to know this bird. Familiar to the point of contemptuousness, the gray jay will steal anything that is not lashed down, whether edible or not. With a little patience on the camper's part, the bird can often be fed from the hand. It is a true omnivore, taking pretty well anything, animal or vegetable. That its diet runs from hamburger meat and baked beans through bacon rinds to soda crackers and licorice all-sorts has been documented.

In the wild, where camp scavenging is not possible, this jay's fare consists of berries, seeds, and fruits, the eggs and nestlings of other birds, and carrion. But the species seems to have "learned" to associate man with food, and no wilderness traveller is without its company for long. With its loose, fluffy plumage, it can fly as silently as an owl, suddenly appearing over one's head as if from nowhere.

When it cares to, the gray jay can be conspicuously noisy. It has as wide an assortment of notes as any Canadian bird – most harsh, but some soft and whistled. Indeed it is such a polygot that when most observers hear a completely unfamiliar note in the evergreen bush, they charge it to the gray jay and let it go at that.

Length 10-13 inches. Male, Rice Lake, Ontario, October.
Immature, The Pas, Manitoba, May.

26

Gray Jay

PERISOREUS CANADENSIS

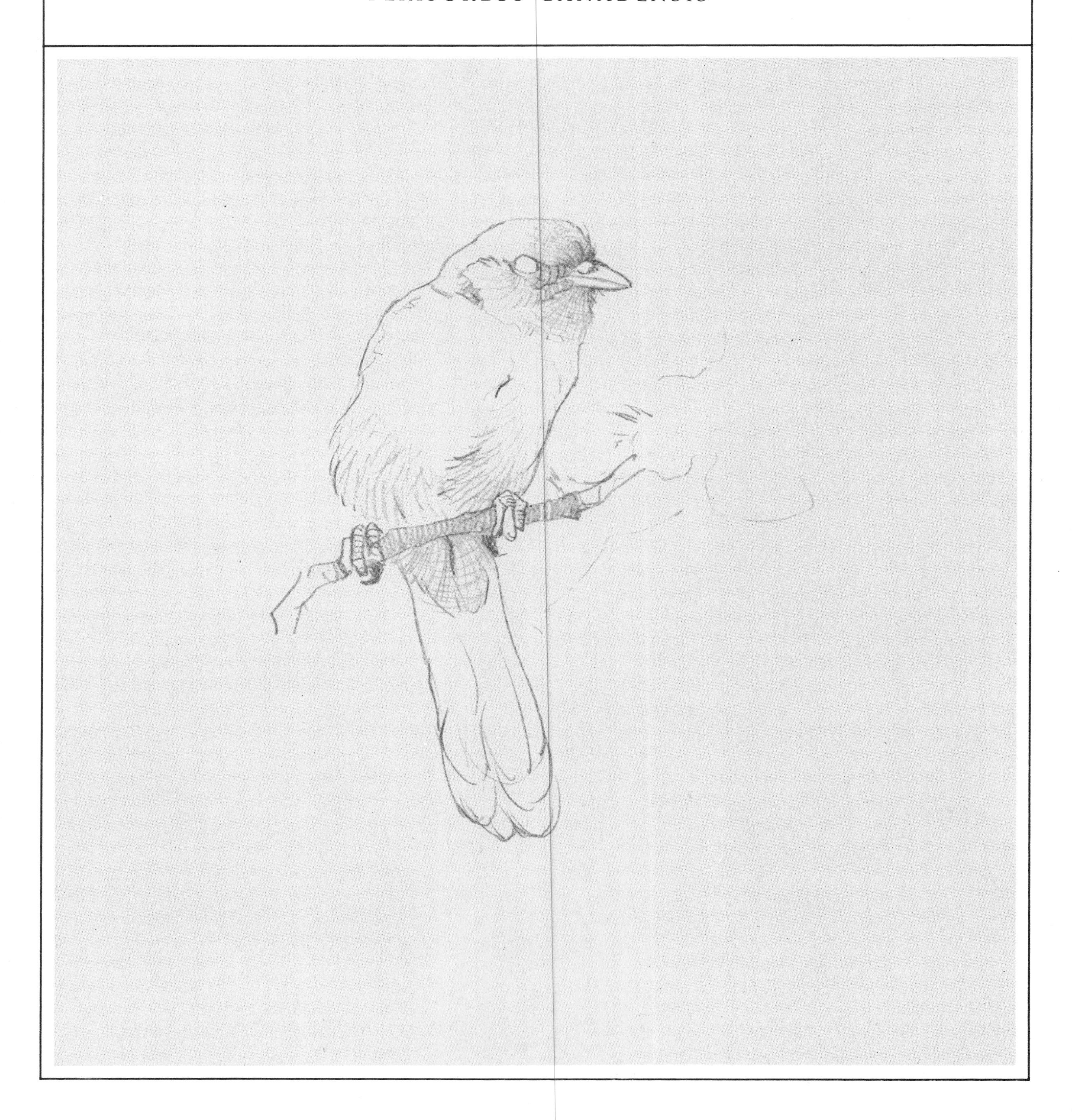

27

Common Raven

CORVUS CORAX

Common Raven - CORVUS CORAX

THE raven is the very embodiment not of evil but of wilderness. In Canada we tend to think of it as a "northern" bird; this is merely because our wilderness happens to be in the north. The bird is found from the arctic to Central America, from the desolate tundra to mountain rock slides, desert canyons, and seacoast cliffs. It is a particularly unsociable animal from man's point of view, and confines itself to the most inaccessible parts of the continent. It occurs also in Europe, Asia, and Africa.

A raven is like a hugely overgrown crow, but there are other differences. Its bill is relatively much longer and stouter; its tail is long and wedge-shaped. In its hawk-like soaring, the flight feathers are widely spread apart, almost like those of a vulture. At close range you can see a shaggy "beard" at the throat. The hoarse croak of the raven is quite unlike the call of a crow.

Like its relatives, the jays, crows, and magpies, the raven will eat pretty nearly anything, including carrion. This taste has been the bird's death warrant in those parts of the continent where predator persecution has involved the barbaric use of baits treated with strychnine, "1080," and other poisons. Massive and insensate campaigns have been mounted against wolves, coyotes, and other animals (always under the euphemistic guise of "control"). This deliberate slaughter has arisen from pressure applied by organized interests such as tourist outfitters, farmers, and ranchers. It has cut terrible swaths not only through the target species but many others as well. Eagles and sundry fur-bearing mammals have been victims as well as the crow family.

Ravens, crows, and jays have always been known to be intelligent birds. That ravens have more than the standard bird brain has been demonstrated in laboratory experiments. The species showed the ability to "count," that is, to distinguish accurately between targets with different numbers of spots on them, and to select the right target when presented with an appropriate cue card. The related Old World rook is known to have a kind of traditional learning process in which symbolic elements such as "language" have been detected. This is probably the most fascinating family of birds.

Length 21½-27 inches. Male, Pefferlaw, Ontario, October.

Boreal Chickadee - PARUS HUDSONICUS

CANADA has six of the world family of sixty-four species of titmice. Known variously as the brown-capped, Columbian, Acadian, and Hudsonian chickadee, this species lives in the great conifer belt from Alaska to New England. Except under the pressure of food shortage, it rarely ventures south of the evergreen forest.

When it does come south, however, it is often in staggering numbers. Remarkable irruptions of this species occur once in a while, resulting in movement far beyond its normal range. Once, great numbers of them invaded the unlikely habitat offered by the glass, steel, and concrete of New York City. In common with certain other birds (waxwings and some finches among them) the titmice may enjoy two or three successive years of unusual prosperity when food is in abundance and living (and thus breeding) is easy. The result is a fast and substantial build-up in population. This offers no problem so long as the food supply is constant. But if a food "crash" should develop next year, due to the vagaries of weather or other factors, great numbers of birds are forced to move much farther south in winter than they normally would.

In most years, however, these birds do not move very far in a latitudinal sense. Small bands of them roam about the coniferous forest in winter, searching for insects and other animal protein as they go. It seems incredible that such minute birds can survive the fearful cold of northern winter, but they do.

No bird migrates south because of the temperature; it migrates to find food. There is plenty of food in the spruce forest in the form of over-wintering insects, their pupae, larvae, and eggs, and the chickadees manage to find it. So long as their metabolic furnaces are well stoked, insulating fat and feathers do the rest.

But a small bird burns up energy at such a high rate that it must eat very often – almost constantly during the short daylight hours of the northern winter. At thirty below zero, a bird that is hungry at nightfall may not survive until morning; a well-fed bird, no matter what the weather, will be warm, active, and efficient when the next day's foraging begins.

Length 5-5½ inches. Male, Pottageville, Ontario, October.

28

Boreal Chickadee

PARUS HUDSONICUS

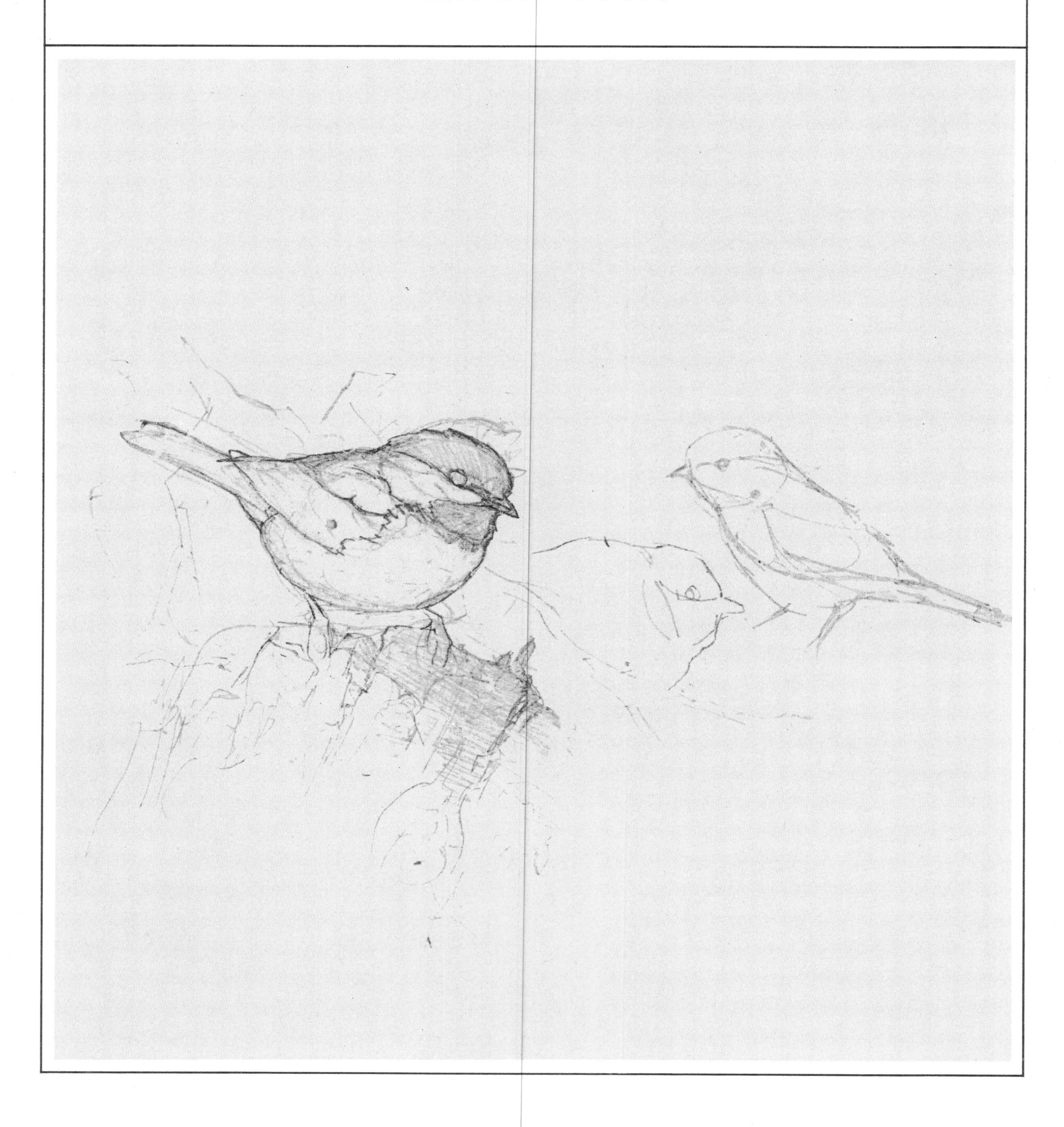

Red-breasted Nuthatch - SITTA CANADENSIS

THE nuthatches are a world-wide family of birds that occur chiefly in the northern hemisphere. The name originated with the European nuthatch, which has been alleged to be able to open hazel nuts (hence "nut-hack"). This small North American species confines itself to much less formidable challenges.

Nuthatches resemble woodpeckers very superficially; they make their way up and down the trunks of trees, digging in the bark for various items of food. But the two families are not related, and there are important differences. A woodpecker props itself against the trunk with its stiff tail, always in a more or less upright position. A nuthatch does not use its short, stubby tail for support, but depends on its feet, which it usually places one above the other. It commonly descends a tree head first, which no woodpecker does. Its long, sharp bill probes deeply into bark crevices and other hiding places of insects, spiders, and other small invertebrates. Occasionally some nuthatches will take to the air to snap up passing insects.

In winter, this common species concentrates for a good part of its food supply on the seeds of various conifers. In years when the cone crop is poor (and especially if the crop has been good in immediately prior years), great flights come south in winter, as with the boreal chickadee. These irruptions are sporadic and unpredictable; they are not on any definable schedule.

For nesting, the bird uses an existing cavity in a spruce or balsam fir (or a pine in the south), or it will excavate one for itself in a rotten conifer. The nest is lined with wood fibres, soft grasses, and shredded bark. Most peculiar is the bird's habit of smearing evergreen pitch around the entrance to the nesting hole. Spruce, fir, or pine pitch is liberally plastered on all bare wood around or near the opening to the cavity – to what purpose, no one knows. An interesting sidelight on this, though not necessarily related to it, is that the nuthatch can fly directly through the hole and into the nest without stopping or even pausing at the rim. How it brakes in time to come to rest inside is an open question.

Length 4½-4¾ inches. Female, Bruce County, Ontario, September.

29

Red-breasted Nuthatch

SITTA CANADENSIS

30

Winter Wren

TROGLODYTES TROGLODYTES

Winter Wren - TROGLODYTES TROGLODYTES

Of the world's sixty-three species of wrens, only this one occurs outside the Americas. The centre of abundance of the wrens is in South America; Canada has only eight species. The winter wren, however, adaptable and venturesome creature that it is, has made its way over the years across the Bering Strait into Siberia; from there it has fanned across Eurasia and North Africa, finally reaching Iceland. Since it is the only wren in the Old World, it is known there as *the* wren, or, more familiarly in Britain, "Jenny" wren.

This is the next-to-smallest of Canadian wrens. With its very stubby tail and dark plumage, and its reluctance to leave the tangled down-timber and mosses of the forest floor, it often resembles a mouse as it darts and scurries about in the security of its almost impenetrable surroundings. Were it not for its song, most times one would never see it.

The song of the winter wren is one of the marvels of the northern forest. It has no characteristic phrase, no definable structure; it is a glorious welter of pure, crystal notes, a formless babble of tinkling expressions so attenuated as to seem endless. It is a particularly high-pitched song; not every listener can pick up all the highest frequencies. But even snatches of it are quite unlike the notes of any other inhabitant of the forest.

In common with many other small birds, wrens are incredibly volatile. Their breeding habits reflect their restless, high-key natures. The male winter wren may build several nests, only one of which may be used. Or, if opportunity arises, he will cheerfully turn polygamist; the extra nests are available for such an eventuality.

The nest is a bulky mass, a structure of mosses and tiny twigs with the entrance usually to one side. It is concealed in tangled roots, under a stump or log, sometimes in a crevice – always very close to the ground. Built as it is of the materials of the forest floor, and nearly always skilfully hidden, it is often very difficult to find.

Despite its name, this species does not winter in most parts of Canada. It migrates to the central and southern states, returning in spring to the great evergreen forest from Newfoundland to Alaska.

Length 4-4½ inches. Male, Fraserdale, Ontario, June.

31

Hermit Thrush

HYLOCICHLA GUTTATA

Hermit Thrush - HYLOCICHLA GUTTATA

THE thrush family is nearly world-wide; it comprises more than three hundred species, of which twelve are found in Canada. It includes the familiar robin, the bluebirds, the wheatear of the arctic and the Townsend's solitaire of the western mountains, in addition to the typical brown thrushes such as those pictured here. In the Old World, such notable vocalists as the European blackbird, the nightingale and the song thrush are all members of this celebrated clan, so richly enjoyed by man since the dawn of his acoustic appreciation.

Thrushes inhabit almost every type of Canadian environment from the great cities and lush deciduous forests of the southeast to the arctic barrens. This species, which in many ways is very like its counterpart the nightingale, breeds from Alaska to Labrador and well down into the United States. Unlike some of its relatives, it is not overly choosy about its habitat, although the majority of hermit thrushes live in the evergreen forest.

This is a quiet, inconspicuous bird that sticks very close to the forest floor. Often the only view granted the observer is a flick of its reddish tail as the bird silently darts through the undergrowth to a more secluded hiding place. But if it is secretive and anonymous during the day, the hermit thrush comes into its own at evening, with a pure, flute-like song that some consider the most beautiful and compelling sound in nature – clear, ethereal, and deliberately phrased. But despite the magnificence of its song, the sound is no give-away to the bird's location; it varies so much in volume and pitch that it is almost impossible to get an accurate fix on the singer. It has been learned that no two individuals sing the same pattern.

The hermit thrush is one of our earlier spring migrants; some years it arrives in southern parts of the country before the snow has entirely gone. It shows a related reluctance to move south in the fall. Though some hermit thrushes winter as far south as Central America, most remain in the southern and central USA, and a few occasionally brave the snows of southwestern Ontario's "banana belt" throughout the winter.

Length 6½-7¾ inches. Male, Chapleau, Ontario, June.

32

Swainson's Thrush

HYLOCICHLA USTULATA

Swainson's Thrush - HYLOCICHLA USTULATA

OVER most of Canada, this species is known as the olive-backed thrush, which would be a much better name if birds of the far west did not have russet backs. As geographically isolated populations of birds often have characteristics distinct from others of their species, it is sometimes difficult on a continent as large as North America to find a descriptive name appropriate to all of a species' local races. So Swainson's thrush it is.

Though it is probably not the equal of the hermit thrush as a singer (what bird is?), this species has much of the musical acomplishment of its family. Its melodious song characteristically spirals upward; that of the related veery, a bird of the southern forest, spirals downward. Like most other brown thrushes, Swainson's usually sings in the evening. During the rest of the day it scarcely utters any sound, and is thus quite awkward to find at the nesting season.

Swainson's thrush breeds from Newfoundland to Alaska and south to the northern tier of states. It is a very widespread and abundant bird over the great reaches of the coniferous forest, favoring low, damp areas near water. It shows a special liking for smaller, young evergreens intermixed with aspens, birches, and other pioneers of second-growth situations.

Like so many other small-to-medium-sized birds, this thrush migrates at night. For the winter, it moves as far south as Peru and Argentina. Most birds that migrate over extremely long distances tend to be blown off course once in a while and to arrive in some unexpected places. Such is the case with Swainson's thrush, which turns up in Europe from time to time.

Though this bird does not look much like our backyard robin in its adult plumage, the relationship of our thrushes is manifest in the markings of the young fledglings, which are heavily spotted. Young thrushes have a way of leaving the nest very early – several days before they can fly. Demands on parental care and watchfulness are thus more onerous than in many other songbird families.

Length 6½-7¾ inches. Male, Nipissing District, Ontario, July.

Gray-cheeked Thrush - HYLOCICHLA MINIMA

THIS is the most northerly of our brown thrushes. It breeds through the boreal forest north to the limit of trees and even beyond. At those places on the edge of the vast tundra where stunted spruce trees give way to dwarf willows and birches, the gray-cheeked thrush will venture out onto the barrens as far as there are shrubs of sufficient size to provide cover for nesting.

Since it shows no reluctance to explore the North, even beyond the tree line, it is not surprising that the gray-cheeked thrush has made its way through Alaska to northeastern Siberia. Yet, when winter comes, these birds do not move southward over the Asian land mass. They return each fall by the route their pioneering ancestors used, moving east over what seems an unnecessarily wide arc of the globe before turning south toward their wintering grounds in the tropics of the West Indies and northern South America. Birds are in more of a traditional "rut" than we (sometimes envious) landbound mammals realize.

The nest of this species is built on the ground or in a tree or shrub, and may be situated as high as twenty feet, depending upon the size of available vegetation. Like its relatives, this thrush is a secretive bird – until it begins to sing. It very rarely sings in migration, and few students have heard it; the song is described as being somewhat like that of a veery, but thinner, higher-pitched, and more nasal.

An interesting phenomenon, unusual among birds, is the contribution of the female to courtship song. Both sexes sing, and the voice of the female is said to be nearly as elaborate as that of the male. The two birds may sing either the same song or a different one; they may sing simultaneously (in duet) or alternately. Other Canadian species in which the females sing include the mockingbird, the cardinal, and the rose-breasted and black-headed grosbeaks. In addition, such birds as the South American jacamars and some of the African barbets, among others, go in for duetting.

The gray-cheeked thrush has an interesting pattern of migration in spring. Instead of rushing the season, as the hermit thrush does, this species tarries and dallies in southern latitudes such as the coast of the Gulf of Mexico until almost the last minute. Then, when conditions in the north are suitable, it moves headlong, accelerating as it goes. By the time it reaches the northern half of the continent, it is moving almost twice as fast as it was in the southern states.

Length 7-8 inches. Male, Sandhill Lake, Manitoba, June.

33

Gray-cheeked Thrush

HYLOCICHLA MINIMA

34

Golden-crowned Kinglet

REGULUS SATRAPA

plate 34

Golden-crowned Kinglet - REGULUS SATRAPA

WITH the exception of certain hummingbirds, kinglets are the smallest North American birds. The European opposite number of this species, the firecrest, is that continent's smallest bird. These minute creatures are members of the Old World warbler family. Presumably they came this way via Siberia and the Bering Strait. But that was very long ago, because the two North American species are no longer identical with their Eurasian relatives; they have changed in the meantime.

This is a very widespread bird, ranging from Alaska east and south to the higher country of South Carolina and Arizona. It winters as far south as the Gulf states, though in general it does not move as far south as the ruby-crowned kinglet. Indeed many birds remain all winter long fairly close to the northern limit of their breeding range. This makes the migrations rather inconspicuous by comparison with those of many other birds.

The golden-crown always nests in a conifer, whether it be a pine, fir, spruce, or hemlock, yet it does not insist upon a pure culture of evergreens in the immediate neighborhood. It likes mixed forest just as long as conifers predominate. Its pendant nest is striking: globular and delicately constructed of mosses, cobwebs, lichens, and bits of leaves. The interior is deeply lined with feathers and has been likened to a cocoon.

This tiny bird lays appropriately tiny eggs, but it produces a lot of them. The average clutch runs to eight or nine, but eleven have been counted. The total weight of a set of eggs may exceed the weight of the bird that laid them! The interior of the nest is small, and in larger clutches the eggs must be deposited in layers so that all may be accomodated.

Natural mortality is high among animals of such fecundity, but the north woods still swarm with golden-crowned kinglets. One is not so much aware of their presence at nesting time as in the off season. Bands of kinglets interspersed with chickadees, nuthatches, woodpeckers, and brown creepers roam the winter woods in an erratic way, sometimes appearing in substantial numbers.

Length 3½-4 inches. Male, Chapleau, Ontario, June.
Female, London, Ontario, April.

35

Ruby-crowned Kinglet

REGULUS CALENDULA

plate 35

Ruby-crowned Kinglet - REGULUS CALENDULA

THIS is rather a drab little bird when compared with the preceding one, but the explosive brilliance of the male's normally concealed crown patch, exposed in moments of high excitement, is thus all the more striking. Like so many of the very smallest birds, kinglets seem to be nearly always in a state of high-key agitation, so one does not usually have to wait long for the ruby crown to be displayed.

Kinglets are constantly in motion, flitting and flickering like moths in the shadows of the evergreen forest, darting one way and another in an incessant search for insect food. Small bodies burn fuel quickly, and most of the kinglet's lifetime is spent in a near frenzy of feeding activity. You never see one sitting around doing nothing; only larger birds can afford that luxury.

As does the golden-crowned, this kinglet nests in coniferous forests across the continent, but it is slightly more northern in summer and slightly more southern in its wintering range. Its migrations are therefore more noticeable than those of its relative. Kinglets migrate at night, and on some spring and autumn mornings the dawn reveals hordes of ruby-crowned mites, all energetically foraging in the trees.

This bird has a harsh, wren-like call note, and seems to "talk" a lot while feeding. It has been suggested that in winter, these notes serve not so much to keep the flock together as to keep individuals *apart*; each bird must have plenty of room to work in if it is to pick up sufficient sustenance in the course of the short winter day.

The golden-crowned kinglet has a thin and undistinguished song, but the ruby-crowned is a noted vocalist. When you happen to be standing close to the bird as it sings, it is almost unbelievable that such a volume of sound could originate in such a wisp of a body. The song is an attenuated, varied, and attractive warble, punctuated by short chatters, and remarkably loud. This is one of the several birds that have voice "dialects" – regional variations in song that are sufficiently different to be characteristic of geographic races or populations.

Nesting is like that of the golden-crowned kinglet. The newly hatched young have been described as being little bigger than bumblebees. Both parents are kept frantically busy feeding the large brood.

Length 3¾-4½ inches. Male, Hamilton, Ontario, May.
Female, Coldstream, Ontario, May.

RUBY CROWNED KINGLET

J.F. LANSDOWNE #35

36

Northern Shrike

LANIUS EXCUBITOR

plate 36

Northern Shrike - LANIUS EXCUBITOR

ALTHOUGH they are true songbirds, the seventy-odd shrikes of the world are highly aberrant ones. They have become adapted to a hawk-like way of life, and have developed somewhat hawk-like physical features to go with it. Shrikes are found chiefly in the Old World; only one, the loggerhead shrike, is confined to this hemisphere. The northern shrike, known in Britain as the great gray shrike, breeds in the subarctic open forest throughout the northern hemisphere, also occurring in North Africa.

This is a fearless, bold, and aggressive bird that has become almost wholly predatory. It lives on the larger insects (when they are available, insects make up a good half of its food), small mammals and birds, reptiles, and amphibians. The bird in the plate has taken a pine siskin. It catches its prey by dropping on it from above and dealing it a decisive blow with its heavy, robust bill. The bill is hooked, with a tooth-and-notch arrangement for a firm grasp in tearing its food.

Its feet and legs, though strong, are not strong enough to capture prey with, in the way a hawk does. Most of the shrike's work is done with its formidable bill. Occasionally it will lodge a victim in the crotch of a twig, or impale it on a thorn. It is not completely clear whether this is merely an aid in holding the meal firm while it is being cut up, or whether it is a deliberate hanging of food. Certainly the bird will return to these carcasses in times of food shortage. It is this habit which gave the shrike the name "butcher-bird" in Britain. Like hawks and owls, it regurgitates indigestible material in the form of pellets.

All predators, the shrike included, are closely tied for survival to the availability of prey. A major part of this species' food consists of voles; voles, like lemmings, experience population build-ups and "crashes" at more or less regular intervals. The four-year cycle of the voles seems to be reflected in concurrent southward flights of northern shrikes in winter.

The shrike hunts in much the same way as small hawks do: by maintaining a vigilant lookout from some good vantage point (in the north, a spruce spire, in the south, a telephone line) and launching itself in swift pursuit of moving prey. The nest is a bulky, somewhat untidy affair in a conifer.

Length 9-10¾ inches. Male, Port Sydney, Ontario, no date.

37

Solitary Vireo

VIREO SOLITARIUS

Solitary Vireo - VIREO SOLITARIUS

PHLEGMATIC, slow-moving, and foliage-coloured, the vireos are some of our least conspicuous birds. The family is unique to the Americas, with its centre of abundance in the tropics. Though they look superficially like warblers, vireos are chunkier in build, much less nimble, and have noticeably stouter (sometimes hooked) bills. They are gleaners of dense, leafy vegetation and go about their work with a measured deliberation that is quite unlike the frenetic activity of the warblers.

This vireo shows a preference for mixed forests, ideally with a good representation of evergreens. Usually it will select one of the latter for nest-building. Its nest is a very neatly constructed basket suspended from a low branch by its upper rim, fashioned with birch bark, mosses, lichens, plant down, and bits of dry leaves and spider silk. The inner lining is of fine grasses and slender rootlets.

The sexes share the duties of incubation, and both appear to sing while on the nest. At this time, the birds are remarkably approachable; they are such close sitters that they will sometimes allow themselves to be touched before flying off the nest. The song is reasonably attractive and varied: a series of short phrases, whistled rather than warbled. But all the vireos make up any deficiency in musical ability with sheer persistence; they are among the most indefatigable of singers.

Since it often builds its nest at a low elevation, this vireo is a common victim of the parasitic brown-headed cowbird, which like the Old World cuckoo lays its eggs in the nests of other birds. It is reported that if the cowbird egg is deposited before any of the vireo's eggs are laid, the bird may cover up the strange intruder and lay her own eggs in the upper storey. If she already has eggs, she will continue to incubate, with the inevitable result – a brood of one lumpy cowbird and no young solitary vireos.

This bird is alternatively called "blue-headed" vireo, but the name "solitary" is also appropriate. It is not a sociable or gregarious bird, and is just as likely to be found migrating with a flock of warblers as it is with its own kind.

Length 5-6 inches. Male, Fraserdale, Ontario, June.

38

Philadelphia Vireo

VIREO PHILADELPHICUS

Philadelphia Vireo - VIREO PHILADELPHICUS

Its name to the contrary, this vireo is a breeding bird of the Canadian forest zone from northern British Columbia to Newfoundland and the upper parts of New England. As so often happens, the bird was described and named from a specimen taken in migration, in this instance at Philadelphia in September 1842.

This is a species that is easily overlooked. It is a night flier in migration, and does not often sing except on the nesting grounds. If possible, it seems to be an even more leisurely feeder than its relatives. Its colour is so much like the surrounding foliage that even when it is in full song it is devilishly hard to spot. Occasionally a sluggish movement will reveal the bird for an instant; if in that instant the plain olive wings (no white bars) and yellowish underparts are evident, its identity is established.

The related red-eyed vireo, a pair of which would seem to inhabit every shade tree north of the southernmost states, has a monotonous robin-like song which is familiar to even the most inexperienced birdwatcher. The voice of the Philadelphia vireo is quite similar, but slower and higher-pitched. It is also something like that of the solitary vireo, but in that species the pacing of the phrases is characteristic. Both sexes appear to incubate and to sing while on the nest.

For nesting, this vireo does not usually select the evergreens of the northern forest, but rather low areas of second growth – sometimes alder thickets or willow jungles, and at others dense stands of young maples. It always demands plenty of leafy cover and usually likes to be near water. The nest itself is like a small cup, neatly woven of lichens, grasses, cobwebs, and birch bark hung from a suitably forked branch.

The origin and evolution of vireos is unclear. Some authorities say they are most closely related to the warblers; others see them as nearer to the shrikes. They behave a good deal like tanagers. But in the time scale of evolution, all of our songbirds are relatively recent. Vireos, warblers, blackbirds, tanagers and finches branched not long ago from the main stream of songbirds and are still, it would seem, in the process of developing new and distinctive characteristics.

Length 4½-5 inches. Male, Rossport, Ontario, June.

39

Tennessee Warbler

VERMIVORA PEREGRINA

Tennessee Warbler - VERMIVORA PEREGRINA

At first glance, this small warbler with its greenish-olive colouration, gray head, and white eye-line might be taken for a vireo. But a second look reveals the fine, sharp bill – needle-thin compared to the stout, curved beak characteristic of the vireos. Above all, its actions distinguish it from the sluggish, deliberate company of vireos. Most warblers are vivacity itself; they are almost constantly on the move in darting, fluttering, nervous activity.

The wood warblers are an American family of some one hundred and fifteen or twenty-odd members, depending upon the authority you consult; forty or so occur in Canada. They are little birds, most of them smaller than sparrows. Many are brightly coloured and boldly patterned; most are energetic if not musical singers on the nesting grounds. Warblers of various kinds range from Alaska and northern Canada to the southern parts of South America, and many are highly migratory. Almost all of them are nearly 100 per cent insectivorous; but, since they must await the right temperatures for hatches of insects, they are not our very earliest migrants in the spring.

Warblers are very widely distributed ecologically; there are few natural environments for which there is not some appropriate warbler species. This is particularly true in the northern Canadian forest, where a wide assortment of these delightful little creatures is enough to guarantee at least one warbler for just about every significant environmental niche.

The Tennessee warbler is not a bird of the deepest evergreen forest; it prefers deciduous and mixed woods and the edges of muskegs and swamps. Its nest is placed on the ground, and is usually made of the north's most ubiquitous commodity, sphagnum. Often this species is remarkably abundant, with many pairs nesting at surprisingly close quarters. The male sings from a high tree; he has a very loud, ringing and emphatic song, with plenty of carrying power. A male is illustrated here; the female is similar, though less contrastingly marked.

The name of the bird clearly has nothing whatever to do with its distribution. The first specimen happened to be taken in Tennessee during migration by Alexander Wilson, the early American ornithologist and bird painter, in 1832.

Length 4½-5 inches. Male, Nakina, Ontario, June.

40

Magnolia Warbler

DENDROICA MAGNOLIA

Magnolia Warbler - DENDROICA MAGNOLIA

THIS magnificent species of the northern evergreen forest got its incongruous name in the same way so many birds did in the early days of American ornithology. It was shot out of a magnolia tree during migration in Mississippi by Alexander Wilson, and named by him in 1811. (It will be remembered that in those days there were no field guides and no museum collections to refer to; identifications had to be made along the barrel of a shotgun.)

There is little doubt, however, that the next time Wilson saw one of these birds, he recognized it. Few warblers are more distinctively marked. Notice especially the black and white tail; it is diagnostic.

Happily for everyone who enjoys birds (who, once exposed to them, cannot?), this is quite a common species that can be seen in numbers during migration. It winters from the West Indies to Panama, moving in April and May to its distant northern breeding grounds, the evergreen forest of Canada. Its typical habitat consists of fairly open stands of white spruce and balsam fir, with the usual admixture of maples and birches. The nest is normally built in a young evergreen; it is a somewhat loose and untidy construction of little twigs and stout grasses lined with fine rootlets.

At the height of the breeding season, the male is an unforgettable sight. In full display, he fans his striking tail to its greatest extent, flashing its black and white pattern, droops the wings to show their white patches, while his breast glows against the sombre backdrop of the evergreens.

Three to five eggs are laid and are incubated only by the female. When they hatch, both parents are kept busy during every moment of daylight to feed the demanding brood. One student closely observed the feeding process, and estimated that the young were fed, on the average, once every four minutes. When one considers the relatively high density of warblers throughout the northern forest, the number of insects taken must be incalculable. During major outbreaks of spruce budworm in the balsam fir country it has been reckoned that warblers have become so common that there was a pair of one species or another every *tenth* of an acre.

Length 4½-5 inches. Female, Caradoc, Ontario, May. Male, Chipewyan, Alberta, June.

41

Black-throated Blue Warbler

DENDROICA CAERULESCENS

Black-throated Blue Warbler - DENDROICA CAERULESCENS

This elegant species is an eastern specialty, breeding between Nova Scotia and Manitoba. Unlike many of the warblers, the sexes are completely different, but the plain female can nearly always be recognized by a tiny white flash in the wing. The male is impossible to confuse with any other bird.

The black-throated blue is not a true northerner; its usual haunts are the deciduous portions of the "transition" zone between the hardwoods and the evergreens. The mixed forest it likes best consists of mature hardwoods such as maple, with a good dense undergrowth of young trees, including conifers. Thus it is frequently found in cut-over areas where natural succession has begun. The nest is placed on or very near the ground in a shrub, small tree, or fallen tree. It is very bulkily made of bits of wood, bark, and leaves, and lined with animal hair and rootlets. Even fine porcupine quills have been reported.

This is a tame and rather slow-moving bird for a warbler. It is readily approached; when the observer gets too close, it will simply move away to a nearby branch, then resume its deliberate feeding. The bird's husky voice, like its actions, is lazy and unhurried. It has a variety of songs, but the throaty quality is usually detectable.

This species and the cerulean warbler of the south are our only two strikingly blue warblers. This colour is not the product of any blue pigment. Blue in the feathering of birds is a structural or mechanical effect. Just as minute particles in the atmosphere scatter out the shorter wave-lengths of visible light and give the sky its blue appearance, tiny air-filled cavities in the feathers of "blue" birds have a screening effect, eliminating from our vision all wave-lengths save the blue. A "blue" bird, soaking wet, looks black; in anything but reflected light, it looks brown.

Length 5-5 1/2 inches. Female, Toronto, Ontario, September.
Male, Elmsdale, Ontario, Spring.

42

Myrtle Warbler

DENDROICA CORONATA

Myrtle Warbler - DENDROICA CORONATA

THIS, the most rugged of our warblers, is exceptional in several ways. It is possibly the most abundant species and is extremely widespread from Newfoundland to Alaska. It is the first warbler to appear in spring, and the last to leave our latitudes in fall; indeed some myrtle warblers winter a surprisingly long way north. This is because, unlike its relatives, this species is not wholly dependent upon insects. It will eat the fruit of trees and shrubs of various kinds, most especially the berries of the wax myrtle, which grows in such profusion in the heart of its wintering range along the coast of the Carolinas.

In spring migration, the bulk of the myrtle warblers come north by way of the valley of the Mississippi; the birds pour up this great flyway in vast numbers during late March and April. Since this is our only warbler that is able to survive low temperatures, it often arrives in southern Canada in chilly weather with the hermit thrushes and fox sparrows.

When they are on the move, myrtle warblers are dogged foragers, creeping about and around twigs, buds, and leaves, sometimes hanging upside down like titmice, and at other times flycatching. In all their quick, darting movements the yellow rump is conspicuous, and an excellent field mark. Note the white throat. In the west (from Cypress Hills, Saskatchewan, to central British Columbia) there lives the very similar and closely related Audubon's warbler. Except for the fact that Audubon's has a yellow throat and a magnolia-like white wing patch, the two birds are almost identical, and very probably were one species not very long ago. Some authorities will suggest that they are the same species today. Hybridization between them is known.

The myrtle warbler nests at rather low elevations in such conifers as white pine, cedar, hemlock, and white spruce. It favours mixed woodlands, but will usually choose an evergreen to nest in. The nest is composed of small twigs laced together into a cup with strips of bark, fibres, and miscellaneous bits of plants. It is lined with fibres and hair.

Length 5-6 inches. Male, Nakina, Ontario, June.
Female, Toronto, Ontario, May.

43

Black-throated Green Warbler

DENDROICA VIRENS

Black-throated Green Warbler - DENDROICA VIRENS

ALTHOUGH it is a moderately striking bird, this smallish warbler is difficult to see, as it haunts the upper storeys of the evergreen forest. It is not at all shy – indeed, often quite confiding – but since it spends so much of its time at the higher levels of the trees, it is as difficult as an insect to pick out among the dense greenery. It is a very active bird, and one is repaid for a stiff neck by an occasional glimpse of bright yellow cheeks outlined by the black throat and dark crown. The female lacks much of the black throat, but the yellow face identifies both sexes.

The song of this species is quite distinctive: a "drowsy" series of "*zee's*" on changing pitches, drifting down from somewhere in the crowns of the tall spruces and balsam firs it usually selects for nesting. Farther south in its range, it favours hemlock. Though it likes to nest in conifers, it will forage in any trees, including stands of aspen, poplar, and white birch.

While it sings and feeds aloft, the black-throated green warbler seems to build its nest at lower elevations. A horizontal limb is selected, and those who have hunted for this delicate little cup report that it would be frustratingly difficult to find were it not for eye-catching strands of white birch bark that are often interwoven in its sides. The eggs are spotted and number four or five.

This warbler does not breed west of the Rocky Mountains. Between the Great Divide and the Pacific, it is replaced by the closely related Townsend's and black-throated gray warblers. Another very near relative is the golden-cheeked warbler, a species confined to a few counties in Texas. There is a decided family resemblance in the songs of these warblers which, aside from their appearance, leads students of bird evolution to speculate that they have emerged as separate species only quite recently.

In migration, warblers have the habit of travelling in mixed flocks in which several species may be included. Rare is the May warbler "wave" in the eastern part of the continent that does not include substantial representation from the black-throated green.

Length 4 1/2-5 1/4 inches. Male, Madge Lake, Saskatchewan, May.

44

Blackburnian Warbler

DENDROICA FUSCA

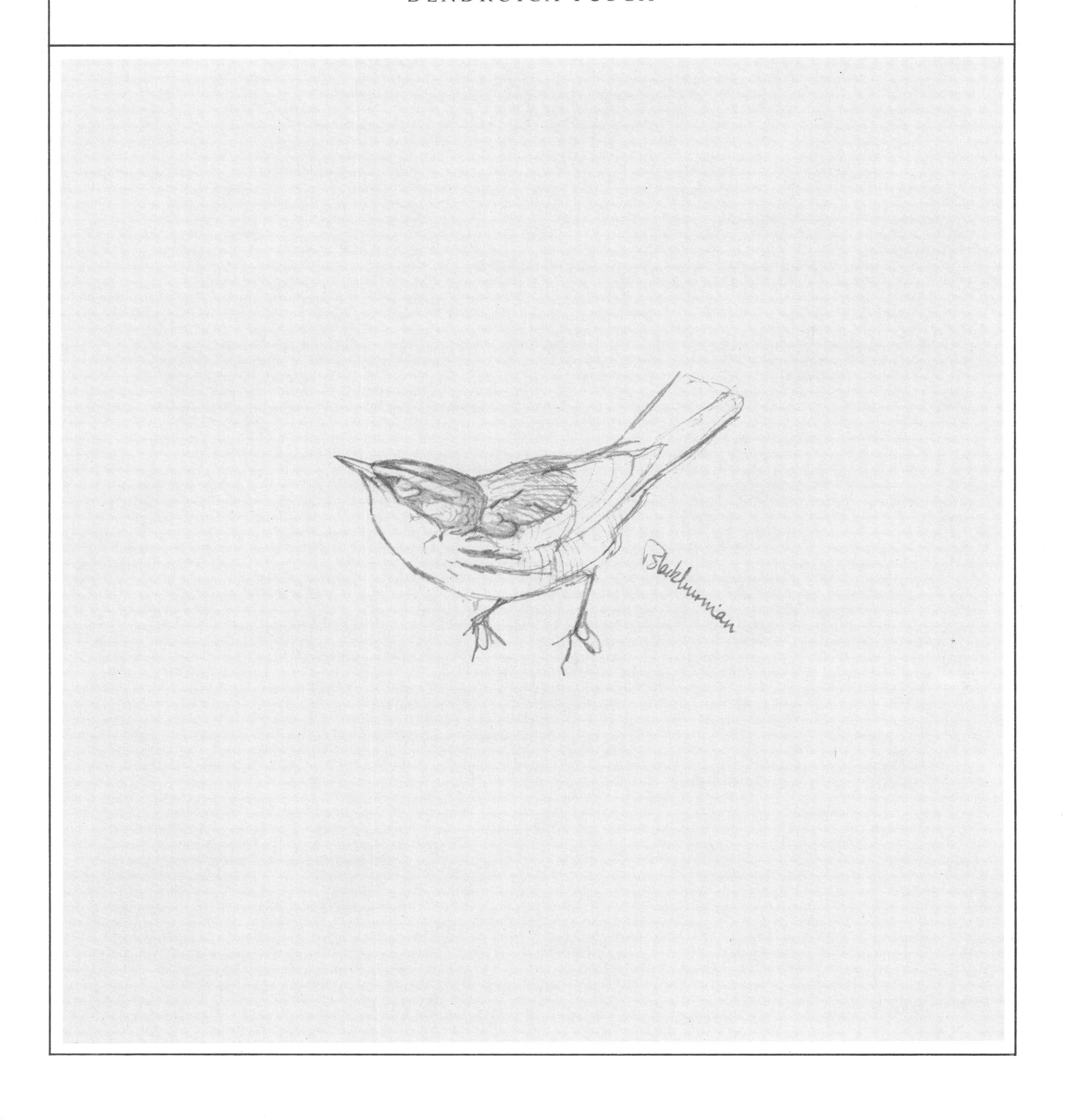

Blackburnian Warbler - DENDROICA FUSCA

THERE is one instance in which the naming of a bird in honour of a person made some (albeit accidental) sense. This bird was named for one Mrs. Blackburn, an Englishwoman who was interested in birds, in the late 18th century. The coincidence is that the bird has much black about it, and as A. C. Bent pointed out, the throat of the male "burns like a brilliant orange flame amid the dark foliage of the hemlocks and spruces." A fair enough outcome.

Except for the almost artificial radiance of the male's throat, this warbler is not a particularly striking one. But its facial pattern is distinctive even in autumn, when the birds have a generally washed-out appearance.

The Blackburnian warbler is essentially an easterner, breeding from Nova Scotia to James Bay and west to Manitoba. A few may spill over into favoured spots on the prairies, but only a very few. In the Appalachians, however, where the mountain ranges supply the necessary altitude for the right evergreens, this warbler nests as far south as South Carolina and Georgia.

In the south, this is a bird of the pines and hemlocks; in the north, it lives in the spruces. In common with many of its relatives, it likes to sing from the topmost spire of a tall dead spruce or hemlock; the high-pitched zippy song drifts earthward so faintly that it might have been caused by some small insect. Just as individual eyesight varies in man, so does hearing; many people have never been able to hear an incredibly thin and wiry upward-sliding note at the end of the song. The onset of human middle age seems to carry with it the loss of most of the extremely high-frequency bird songs: this one, that of the blackpoll, the bay-breasted, parts of the winter wren's, and several more. For the student interested in warblers, this is bad news, since so many of them (the Blackburnian included) are so many times more often heard than seen. The dense canopy of the forest is ample concealment for these diminutive birds.

The nest may be situated almost anywhere in a conifer (there are records of nests found at from five to eighty feet), but higher levels are most usual. Twigs, plant down of various kinds and *Usnea* lichen are fashioned into a graceful cup which is lined with hair, fine grass, and rootlets.

Length 4½-5½ inches. Male, Hamilton, Ontario, May.
Female, Long Point, Ontario, May.

45

Bay-breasted Warbler

DENDROICA CASTANEA

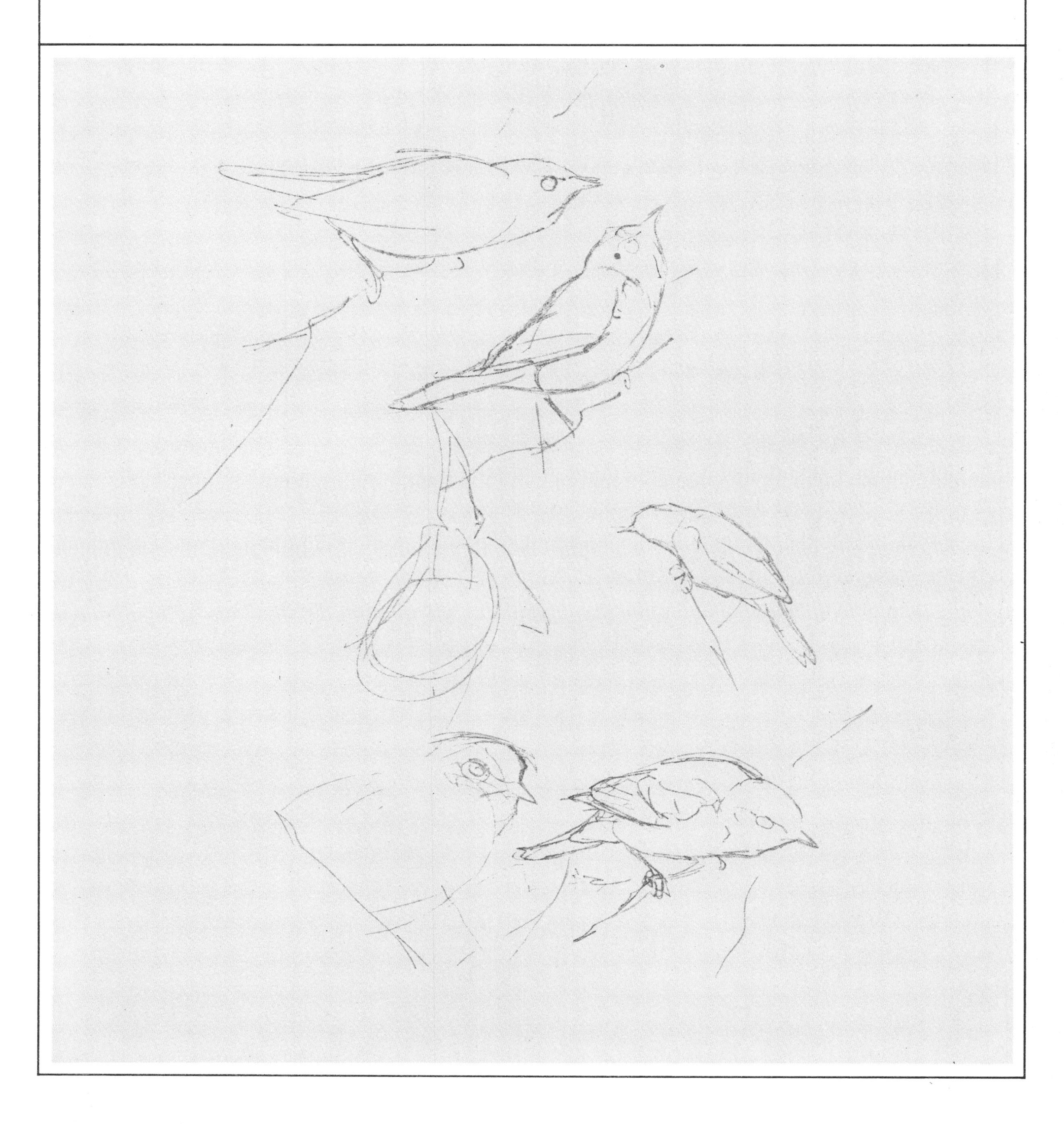

Bay-breasted Warbler - DENDROICA CASTANEA

IN a family in which at least some degree of flamboyance in plumage is the general rule, the male bay-breasted warbler is the soul of impeccable good taste. It even wears a pale stiff collar round its neck, which is the best field mark on an otherwise dark, somewhat hefty warbler.

Normally this is not a terribly common bird, by the standards set by some of the other warblers. Yet given the opportunity by favourable nesting conditions and an abundance of food, it can increase to surprising levels. In areas of heavy spruce budworm infestation, its population has been known to rise spectacularly, to the extent that in one such area, eighty-eight pairs of bay-breasted warblers were counted; their territories averaged slightly more than one-third of an acre per pair – a remarkable density for any such songbird.

This is an excellent example of the way in which the economics of nature manage to respond to unusual conditions – outbreaks of one species are balanced, or compensated for, by increases in another. Chemical pesticides reduce both insects and birds drastically – but neither completely. The budworm in particular seems able to pop up again in another part of the forest without much loss of time.

Though it looks so different, this species is very closely related to the blackpoll warbler, which is a much more common bird. This relationship is not evident in the plumage of adult males in spring, but in the autumn the two species (especially the young birds) are indistinguishable to the untrained eye. There *are* differences, however, for which the reader is referred to Roger Tory Peterson's *Field Guide to the Birds*. The familial ties of these two species are apparent also in the fact that they have been known to hybridize.

The song of the bay-breasted warbler is quite monotonous for a member of its family. It is a very high-pitched, sibilant, and thin series of two-syllable notes on the same pitch, not always readily picked up by the inexperienced ear.

This is one of the last migrant warblers to come through southern Canada in spring. But it has a long way to travel: from Panama and Venezuela all the way to the boreal forest stretching from Newfoundland and Labrador to Alaska.

*Length 5-6 inches. Female, Lake Attawapiskat, Ontario, June.
Male, Caradoc, Ontario, May.*

46

Blackpoll Warbler

DENDROICA STRIATA

Blackpoll Warbler - DENDROICA STRIATA

It is a long, long way from the tropics of South America to the Canadian timber-line, but the blackpoll manages this great journey each spring and fall with no apparent difficulty. It is one of the very last warblers to pass through populated Canada on the way north; when the blackpolls appear, the wonderful migration of the warblers is drawing to an end.

The schedule of its northern flight is interesting. The wintering grounds are in Guiana, Brazil, and Peru. From there it moves to Venezuela and across the chain of the West Indies, via Cuba, to Florida. It generally reaches the Florida mainland about April 20, and does not arrive at the latitude of the Great Lakes until May 15 to 20, representing a month more or less for that leg of the journey. Then the flight speeds up. In another ten days or two weeks (or May 30), the birds have arrived on their northern breeding grounds from Newfoundland to Alaska.

At the start of its migration, the blackpoll is moving at the rate of about thirty miles per day; at the end, it is doing two hundred miles per day. This rapid acceleration has been noted in several birds, including the gray-cheeked thrush, which occupies the same far northern environment at the limit of trees. If it is measured in a straight line, the greatest extent of this fantastic trip of the blackpoll adds up to five thousand miles, one way. But it is *not* in a straight line, and it is anyone's guess how much more than ten thousand miles an individual bird may fly in one year.

The blackpoll in spring plumage can only be confused with the black-and-white warbler, but the latter has its crown broken by a white stripe, and it spends most of its time in an un-warbler-like creeping up and down tree trunks. The female blackpoll lacks the black cap. In fall, the blackpoll looks like a totally different bird – very, very like the bay-breasted warbler. At that season the blackpolls move in small flocks; in the spring they are more solitary and seem to travel singly or in groups of two or three. They are not quite so hyper-active as most other warblers, and methodically work spring willow and alder catkins as the migration proceeds.

The song of the blackpoll is excruciatingly high-pitched and thin; one often has to make a deliberate effort to tune in on its frequency before it can be picked up. The average frequency has been worked out at 8,900, "over an octave above the highest tone on the piano"; it can reach 10,225.

Length 5-5 3/4 inches. Male, Kinglet Lake, Quebec, July.

47

Palm Warbler

DENDROICA PALMARUM

Palm Warbler - DENDROICA PALMARUM

WHY a breeding bird of the northern Canadian forest should have the word "palm" attached to it will become evident when the birdwatcher visits Florida in the winter. He will spend a good deal of time checking local warblers (which are abundant) until he realizes that almost every other bird he looks at is this species. To be absolutely accurate about it, however, the bird does not frequent the palm trees; it seems to be everywhere else *but*. Nonetheless, the name does evoke a picture of that subtropical environment characteristic of half of the bird's life story.

For the other half of the year, this is a bird of the black spruce and jack pine forests of the north and northwest. It likes heavily wooded areas in the southern part of its range, and builds its nest of mosses and grasses on the ground. Farther north, in the subarctic, it nests in the open muskegs where there are scattered spruces and tamaracks.

Unlike most *Dendroica* warblers, this one spends much of its time on the ground, whether on the asphalt of a Florida parking lot or on the sphagnum of the north. It is a conspicuous bird, not only because of its tame and fearless nature, but also because of its habit of perpetually bobbing and wagging its tail up and down. This constant flicking can become an annoyance to the birdwatcher (who by definition has sensitive peripheral vision); try as he will, he cannot help instinctively turning his head to check some movement caught in the corner of one eye. It's always the palm warbler again.

The sexes are similar. In spring, the best marks are the chestnut cap, yellow under the tail, general colouration, and the movements of the tail. Fall birds do not have the conspicuous cap. Like those of so many of its immediate relatives, the palm warbler's voice is thin, weak, and undistinguished, consisting of a repetitious series of six or seven unmusical and sibilant notes, all on one pitch.

There are two well-defined races or subspecies of the palm warbler in Canada. One ranges from the Great Lakes to Hudson Bay and the Mackenzie, the other from the Great Lakes and James Bay east to Newfoundland, Nova Scotia, and northern New England. The western form is illustrated here.

Length 4½-5½ inches. Male, Favourable Lake, Ontario, June.

48

Northern Waterthrush

SEIURUS NOVEBORACENSIS

plate 48

Northern Waterthrush - SEIURUS NOVEBORACENSIS

THE unusual warbler genus *Seiurus* includes three species that are anything but warbler-like: the well-known ovenbird of the southern forests and two kinds of waterthrushes. "Waterthrush" may or may not be an inapropriate vernacular name; certainly the birds are warblers, not thrushes, but they *look* like thrushes and they definitely like the water.

This species and the very similar Louisiana waterthrush (a bird of the southern forest which barely trickles into Canada) may be distinguished most easily by the colour of the eyebrow stripe. In this species, it is buffy; in the Louisiana, it is white. The ovenbird has an orange crown on its head which is unmistakable.

All three of these ground-frequenting warblers *walk*, instead of hopping. No other warbler does this. Even the palm warbler, which is commonly seen on the ground, never walks. The waterthrushes stride up and down the margins of pools and streams "like mechanical toys," as Peterson describes it, and have the curious habit of bobbing, teetering, and tilting up and down in the way of a spotted sandpiper.

This is a bird of shaded swamps and bogs, favouring deep shrubby tangles at the water's edge. In the heavy underbrush, it maintains a constant search for small aquatic animals – such things as insects, worms, and tiny crustaceans – by poking under wet logs, leaves, bits of sodden bark, and mud. Its song is one of the memorable features of the wet woods. It is very loud, emphatic, and ringing, with clearly enunciated and rapidly accelerating phrases, carrying for considerable distances through the dense understorey. (Many birds of the very deep forest have loud, ringing voices of remarkable carrying power; this is especially true in tropical jungles.)

There is plenty of water in the great northern forest, and thus there is ample habitat for the waterthrush. It is distributed pretty well countrywide, from the southern border to the limit of trees. It is also found in appropriately cool and shady retreats in the northern parts of the USA.

Length 5½-6½ inches. Male, Favourable Lake, Ontario, May.

49

Rusty Blackbird

EUPHAGUS CAROLINUS

plate 49

Rusty Blackbird - EUPHAGUS CAROLINUS

In the Old World, the blackbird is a thrush, very like the American robin. In the Americas, the endemic blackbird family includes many of our most brilliant birds, including the bobolink and meadowlarks, orioles and troupials, caciques and oropendolas, as well as the *black* blackbirds with which nearly everyone is familiar – redwings, grackles, and others. The centre of blackbird abundance is in the tropics; only twelve of the eighty-eight species occur in Canada.

Here is a kind of "oriole," then, that breeds inside the Arctic Circle – the northernmost of its family. Unlike the other black blackbirds, this species shows a strong affinity for water; as often as not its nest will be built beside or even over the water in the trees and shrubs surrounding a forest pond, stream, or bog. Most of our other blackbirds do not care for thickly wooded areas. The rusty nests as far north as the limit of trees and as far south, where habitat permits, as northern New England.

Most blackbirds are gregarious, especially during migration. Massed mixed flocks of redwinged blackbirds, grackles, and cowbirds are familiar to every birdwatcher; this species, though it flocks just as tightly, seems to prefer its own company. It is less likely to mingle with the others. The great spring flight, in which remarkably dense and compact flocks may be seen, begins in the southern states in March and reaches the Great Lakes in April. By May the birds have reached their breeding grounds in the immensity of the wet boreal forest. Only during the nesting period does the rusty blackbird become a solitary species. Soon after the young are on the wing, the flocks, bands, and great companies of birds begin to re-assemble.

The bird gets its name from the rusty-brown winter plumage. The amount of colour is variable among individuals and age groups; it is thought to be brightest in young birds. The bird turns glossy black (slate gray for females) in spring by the simple expedient of losing the rusty tips of its feathers, which break off; underneath, they are the proper breeding colour.

Length 8½-9¾ inches. Male, Hamilton, Ontario, October.
Male, Coldstream, Ontario, May.
Female, Fort Albany, Ontario, June.

50

Evening Grosbeak

HESPERIPHONA VESPERTINA

Evening Grosbeak - HESPERIPHONA VESPERTINA

NON-BIRDWATCHERS frequently ask what in the world people of our persuasion find to look at in the wintertime. They may be assured that few sights in nature are more arresting than a flock of evening grosbeaks in clear winter sunlight. Their rich plumage has an almost unreal golden glow against glaring snow and the deep blue January sky. That is the season when most Canadians see this splendid bird; at breeding time it withdraws to the remote wilderness of the boreal forest.

The great, stout, conical bill is a beautiful adaptation to seed-eating; it is reminiscent of that of the Old World hawfinch. In summer, on the breeding areas, evening grosbeaks depend to a great extent on softish buds and berries. It is in winter that the specialized beak really comes into its own. Flocks of the birds descend on such trees as the Manitoba maple (box elder), devouring the winged seeds in amazing quantities with amazing speed. Also, in their winter wanderings, grosbeaks are easily attracted to feeding stations.

In *The Birds of Nova Scotia*, Robie W. Tufts has described the evening grosbeaks' feeding technique. "It is interesting to watch them at close range – eight to ten inches – on the window-tray, clipping the edges off sunflower seeds in order to extract the meat. It is done with marked dexterity. Their powerful bills are like shears, the sharp edges of the upper mandible coming down neatly over the side of the lower one, the seed being manipulated by the tongue."

The bill can also be an effective instrument of defence. The bird bander who handles one of these finches carelessly runs the risk of a nip that he will not soon forget. These grosbeaks are sturdy, bellicose birds, and at feeding stations they do not encourage the company of other species, although some lesser fry such as chickadees, nuthatches, and juncos are tolerated. Competitors such as the pine grosbeak, whose winter diet is similar in some respects, nearly always come off second best.

This is a western bird in terms of breeding abundance, but in the off season there is a tendency for it to move eastward. Birds banded in northern Michigan, for example, moved in the autumn not to the south but almost due east to the Atlantic states of New England. Like the boreal chickadee and others, the evening grosbeak experiences periodic population peaks which bring great numbers into southern latitudes. This does not happen on any sort of timetable comparable to the cycle of the northern shrike; it is sporadic and unpredictable.

Length 7-8½ inches. Female, Rainy River, Ontario, June.
Male, Strickland, Ontario, June.

51

Purple Finch

CARPODACUS PURPUREUS

Purple Finch - CARPODACUS PURPUREUS

THIS is another of the northern finches with which most people are familiar chiefly in winter, when with several of its relatives it readily patronizes home feeding stations. When a small flock of these erratic wanderers visits a backyard tray of millet seeds, sometimes it is overlooked. The females and young birds look very like some kind of undistinguished sparrows; it is not until a raspberry-red male appears that the flock catches our attention. Usually the fully adult males are considerably outnumbered. There may be more males than one suspects, however, for it takes more than one year for them to reach high plumage, and the males are sexually mature and do breed while still in the "female" garb.

The purple finch is one of the more attractive singers of its family. The song is a highly variable, liquid warble and the bird is a very persistent singer, even in winter. The call note is a short, dull, and metallic *tick*, distinctive enough to immediately draw one to the window overlooking the feeding station.

Males on their breeding territories in summer like to sing from chosen perches high in the tops of evergreens. Often, carried away in the enthusiasm of his courtship, a singing male will flutter from his perch, continuing in full song as he describes an aerial "dance" to his own accompaniment. Song is at its best during morning and evening hours.

Its preferred habitat is forest edge – places where the dense evergreen cover is interrupted by standing or running water or by beaver meadows and the scars of old fires. But there must be evergreens of one kind or another. This is the same country occupied by the goshawk, spruce grouse, hawk-owl, three-toed woodpecker, and the long list of warblers and finches – the great transcontinental belt of conifers that parallels the tundra to the north.

Wintering purple finches sometimes move farther than many of their summertime neighbours, migrating as far as the Gulf states in some years. But, like the others, their wanderings are informal; they are common or even abundant one year, scarce or absent the next, which is one of the charms of so many of the northern birds.

Length 5½-6¼ inches. Female, Strathroy, Ontario, December.
Male, Fort Albany, Ontario, July.

52

Pine Grosbeak

PINICOLA ENUCLEATOR

plate 52

Pine Grosbeak - PINICOLA ENUCLEATOR

Our largest finch is also one of the most appealing, with a variety of attractive plumages, a gentle and tolerant disposition, and a pleasant musical voice. It is widely distributed throughout the boreal forest of the northern hemisphere, but only occasionally is it seen in numbers. Like those of so many of the breeding birds of the far north, its appearances in settled areas are unheralded and unscheduled, but they are worth waiting for.

As with the purple finch, fully adult males in their distinctive rose-red plumage are nearly always in the minority when winter flocks visit our latitudes. Sub-adult males are like the females, except that dashes of red make their coloured areas more orange than the dull yellow of the females. Red colouring in these birds is apparently a dietary product; the bird synthesizes red pigment from the contents of the food it eats. Birds raised in captivity often lack the colouration of wild birds.

This is a big, robust bird almost the size of a robin, but it shows some disinclination to tangle with more aggressive species such as the evening grosbeak; although their food habits are somewhat similar, the two species are not often seen together.

Its favoured nesting locations, like those of the purple finch, are the edges and borders of openings in the coniferous forest. Often its nest will be found near water. Buds and seeds are the staple diet; when they come south in winter the birds concentrate on beech nuts and conifer seeds of all kinds. They have also been observed to eat the berries of deadly nightshade (*Belladonna*) with no apparent ill effect.

Nesting pairs keep their distance from each other, but after broods are able to fly, the grosbeaks become gregarious once again, feeding in loose flocks as they aimlessly meander about the forest in late summer. They do not move south as a matter of course; only a food shortage can drive them out of the coniferous zone in any numbers. But when the supply of seeds and berries shrinks, as it occasionally does, the birds move southward, flying by day, to more promising surroundings. When they are on the move, their sweet whistles and deeply undulating, "roller-coaster" flight are reliable field marks.

Length 9-10 inches. Male, Toronto, Ontario, November.
Female, Toronto, Ontario, March.
Immature, Lake St. Martin, Manitoba, October.

53

Pine Siskin

SPINUS PINUS

Pine Siskin - SPINUS PINUS

Here is one of our smallest finches – a dark, heavily-streaked little bird that may or may not show a certain amount of yellow in its wings and at the base of the tail. Its most noticeable features are its extreme gregariousness and its unpredictably nomadic nature. Small flocks and very large flocks appear one day and vanish the next, never seeming to pop up in one place twice running. The same is true of their populations; in some years they are extraordinarily abundant, in others there will be scarcely one to be seen.

The siskin's closest relative is the much more familiar goldfinch, and the two birds have many things in common. In flight, they both undulate markedly; a tightly-packed flock announces its coming before you can properly see it, with light, twittering flight notes more or less in rhythm with the birds' bouncy progress. In winter, both species like open fields with the seed heads of thistles, dandelions, and other annual plants, and they often join foraging companies of redpolls and crossbills. Goldfinches, however, do not usually build up flocks as large as those of the siskins. When the latter arrive in numbers, those numbers are substantial.

Except when they invade lower latitudes, siskins are birds of the transcontinental evergreen forest and the coniferous slopes and valleys of the western mountains. In summer, their food is mixed: insects of various sorts, buds, and small, tender leaves. Seeds are taken at all seasons, especially those of conifers, alders, and birches. Nesting is in the upper storeys of a tall evergreen. Nestlings of both members of this genus are said to be fed in part by the regurgitation of masses of very small seeds, which may be partially pre-digested.

It is often noted by naturalists that several of the northern finches (including this species, the purple finch, pine grosbeak, crossbills, and others), demonstrate a special fondness for salt. It is a common experience, when you are driving along a country gravel road in winter, to flush small flocks of finches from the bare-scraped shoulders of the road. They are presumably picking up grit, but they also seem to have been attracted by salt deposited by highway crews. The significance of this taste is not understood.

Length 4½-5¼ inches. Female, The Pas, Manitoba, June.

54

White-winged Crossbill

LOXIA LEUCOPTERA

White-winged Crossbill - LOXIA LEUCOPTERA

The great world family of finches, including some four hundred and twenty-five species, is considered to be the most recently evolved group of birds. Among other things, they are characterized by stout, wedge-shaped bills, especially useful for seed-cracking. Though crossbills are true finches, they have developed a further and unique refinement of the bill to allow them to specialize in dealing with evergreen cones, one of the toughest forms of plant food for birds to handle.

The parrot-like mandibles of these birds actually cross at their tips, like a miniature pair of ice tongs. When the bird is not eating, its bill would appear to be the very epitome of awkwardness; it is difficult to imagine how an animal with such an overdeveloped bit of anatomy could possibly survive. In practice, it is a beautifully functioning tool that enables the crossbill to do in an instant what another species might take minutes or hours to accomplish, if indeed it could do it at all.

The bill is opened to its fullest extent as the bird bites into a hard evergreen cone. As it is closed, the tips come together and pass one another, scissors-like, resulting in a form of wedge, or lever, that spreads apart the scales of the cone. The bill, now behind a seed, forces it out; the kernel is extracted with the tongue. As simple as shucking peas, if you're a crossbill.

Quite obviously, this bird and its cousin the red crossbill are dependent upon the annual crop of evergreen cones. But the crop is variable from year to year and from place to place. The erratic, nomadic behaviour of both crossbills is probably yet another adaptation to the pressures of their environment. If they were not confirmed wanderers, they might fail to find alternative sources of food supply in poor years. But since they do have such a tendency to move around almost constantly in the non-breeding season, they are able to find suitable feeding grounds even if the cone crop has been thin over a reasonably large area.

In the great coniferous forest, crossbills concentrate on native spruces and balsam firs. When they move south, they feed on hemlocks and the Norway spruces so widely introduced in farming country.

Length 6-6¾ inches. Male, James Bay, Ontario, June.
Female, Murrilo, Ontario, July.

55

Fox Sparrow

PASSERELLA ILIACA

Fox Sparrow - PASSERELLA ILIACA

THOUGH unobtrusive and wary, this large and handsome sparrow has several distinctions. It is a splendid singer; it is important to students of the evolution of bird species; it is a constant challenge to the alertness of the birdwatcher because of its secretive habits.

The fox sparrow nests as far north as there are trees and from ocean to ocean. It reaches the tree limit in the high mountains as well as in the subarctic; it moves upward just as far as there is undergrowth to accommodate it. This is a bird of the thickets, whether they are dense stands of willow and alder along the banks of streams, or shrubby, young or stunted evergreens.

This bird has made a specialty out of living on the ground. It forages there industriously and vigorously, kicking and lashing out with both feet as it sends leaves flying in all directions and explores the rich humus beneath. Like another ground-dwelling finch, the towhee, this sparrow makes far more fuss, noise, and commotion among the leaves than any bird its size properly should. But despite all this, the bird is unusually shy and self-effacing, and it is by no means easy to observe.

The fox sparrow has one of the better voices and, unlike some, readily sings during migration. We may not be favoured always with the complete song, which the bird usually reserves for its nesting territory, but even the abridged version which we hear in southern latitudes is one of the most rewarding experiences of early spring. The full song is pure virtuosity – rich, musical, and varied; in a way, it is reminiscent of the orchard oriole, but infinitely more lyric.

There are a number of races, or subspecies, of fox sparrows. These have been the subject of much study, particularly on the Pacific coast. It has been found that these races never intermingle, not even on migration or on their wintering quarters. Thus, even at a season when they are not geographically isolated as they are at breeding time, the behaviour of the birds keeps the populations separate and distinct. One day, some of these races may become new species, as different from other fox sparrows as song sparrows are today.

Length 6¼-7¼ inches. Male, Sandhill Lake, Manitoba, June.

56

Lincoln's Sparrow

MELOSPIZA LINCOLNII

Lincoln's Sparrow - MELOSPIZA LINCOLNII

THIS very unobtrusive but attractive finch is often mistaken for its much more familiar cousin, the song sparrow. In comparison with its relative, especially in terms of behaviour, it is a most inconspicuous bird, but on close inspection it is anything but drab. It is an unusually tidy and trim little species, finely streaked, with a distinct yellowish-buff band across the breast.

Birds that habitually skulk in the undergrowth as this one does, often pass through in migration largely unnoticed, even though they may be in some numbers. Lincoln's sparrow frequents the densest brushy tangles and thickets on the forest floor, and rarely favours the observer with a good crisp view. This apparent desire for complete anonymity extends to its singing as well; it does not sing in migration to nearly the extent that many of its close relatives do.

This is an extremely widespread sparrow, ranging from Alaska to the lower peninsula of Michigan. In that vast area, only three races or subspecies have been recognized. This is in striking contrast to the ubiquitous song sparrow, of which no less than thirty-one different forms have been described at one time or another. The sexes are alike in plumage, and after the first proper moult the young birds resemble their parents.

The bird is no less secretive on its breeding grounds than it is on migration. For nesting, it chooses low areas such as wet beaver meadows, bogs, and swamps and the borders of lakes, ponds, and creeks. It likes the thickly tangled alder and willow growth in such situations – much the same habitat that is used by the northern waterthrush, among others. In the wide reaches of the boreal forest, wherever impenetrable shrubbery surrounds a marsh or muskeg, there Lincoln's sparrow will be furtively raising its brood of four or five nestlings.

It is a fine singer, delivering a quality somewhere in between that of a purple finch and a house wren; its lively, liquid song is filled with spirit and warmth. The singing perch is usually in a shrub or small tree, but when it is not in voice, the bird inevitably returns to the shaded security of ground level.

Length 5-6 inches. Farquier, Ontario, June.

Bibliography and Index

Bibliography

The birdwatcher is blessed with an extremely wide range of reading, ranging from books especially for the beginner to the vast advanced literature of ornithology. The selection of titles presented here does not pretend to be more than a sample of the sources available; it is offered merely as an introduction to the subject, and includes both elementary and more advanced references. It includes those sources most frequently consulted by the author over the years. Many of the volumes listed contain substantial bibliographies.

Identification

PETERSON, ROGER TORY, *A Field Guide to the Birds*. Boston: Houghton Mifflin, 1947. *A Field Guide to Western Birds*. Boston: Houghton Mifflin, 1961.

POUGH, RICHARD H., *Audubon Land Bird Guide*. Garden City: Doubleday, 1946. *Audubon Water Bird Guide*. Garden City: Doubleday, 1951. *Audubon Western Bird Guide*. Garden City: Doubleday, 1957.

These books are visual aids to bird identification. In many cases, however, the song or call note of a bird may serve as corroboration of a sighting, and occasionally may be even more important than the appearance of a bird. A number of long-play bird recordings of excellent quality has appeared in recent years, and the number is growing. Some are collections of birds of geographic regions; others contain families of birds. For details, the reader is referred to the Federation of Ontario Naturalists, Don Mills, Ontario, Canada.

General and Reference

AMERICAN ORNITHOLOGISTS' UNION, *Check-list of North American Birds* (5th edition). Baltimore: A.O.U., 1957.

AUSTIN, OLIVER L. JR., *and* ARTHUR SINGER, *Birds of the World*. New York: Golden Press, Inc., 1961.

BENT, ARTHUR C., *Life Histories of North American Birds* (20 vols.). Washington: United States National Museum, 1919-1958.

BERGER, ANDREW J., *Bird Study*. New York: John Wiley & Sons, Inc., 1961.

CRUICKSHANK, ALLAN *and* HELEN, *1001 Questions Answered About Birds*. New York: Dodd, Mead & Company, Inc., 1958.

DARLING, LOIS *and* LOUIS, *Bird*. Boston: Houghton Mifflin Company, 1962.

DORST, JEAN, *The Migrations of Birds*. Boston: Houghton Mifflin Company, 1963.

FISHER, JAMES, *and* PETERSON, ROGER TORY, *The World of Birds.* Garden City: Doubleday & Company, Inc., 1963.

FORBUSH, E. H., *and* MAY, JOHN B., *A Natural History of the Birds of Eastern and Central North America.* Boston: Houghton Mifflin Company, 1939.

GRISCOM, L., *and* SPRUNT, A., *The Warblers of North America.* New York: The Devin-Adair Co., 1957.

HICKEY, J. J., *A Guide to Bird Watching.* New York: Oxford University Press, 1943.

KORTRIGHT, F. H., *Ducks, Geese and Swans of North America.* Washington: American Wildlife Institute, 1942.

PETERSON, ROGER TORY *(ed.), The Bird Watcher's Anthology.* New York: Harcourt, Brace & Company, Inc., 1957.

PETERSON, ROGER TORY *and* THE EDITORS OF "LIFE," *The Birds.* New York: Time Inc., 1963.

PETTINGILL, OLIN SEWALL JR., *(ed.), The Bird Watcher's America.* New York: McGraw-Hill Book Company, 1965.

THOMSON, A. LANDSBOROUGH *(ed.), A New Dictionary of Birds.* London: Nelson, 1964.

Canadian

GODFREY, W. EARL, *The Birds of Canada.* Ottawa: National Museum of Canada, (in press 1966).

MUNRO, J. A., *and* COWAN, IAN MCTAGGART, *A Review of the Bird Fauna of British Columbia.* Victoria, B.C. Provincial Museum, Special Publication no. 2, 1947.

PETERS, H. S., *and* BURLEIGH, T. D., *The Birds of Newfoundland.* St. John's, Newfoundland Department of Natural Resources, 1951.

SALT, W. RAY, *and* WILK, A. L., *The Birds of Alberta.* Edmonton, Alberta Department of Economic Affairs, 1958.

SNYDER, L. L., *Ontario Birds.* Toronto: Clarke, Irwin and Company Limited, 1950.

SQUIRES, W. AUSTIN, *The Birds of New Brunswick.* Saint John: The New Brunswick Museum (Monographic Series no. 4), 1952.

TAVERNER, P. A., *Birds of Canada.* Ottawa: Canadian Department of Mines Bulletin no. 72, 1934.

TUFTS, ROBIE W., *The Birds of Nova Scotia.* Halifax: Nova Scotia Museum, 1961.

Index

NOTE: "Page" numbers refer to introduction, "plate" numbers to main text.
Numbers in italic denote accompanying illustration

On the Making of this Book

This book was planned and designed by Frank Newfeld

The type chosen is Palatino,
a design created by Hermann Zapf for
Stempel Linotype, Frankfurt, and first issued in 1950.
It is a Roman face with broad letters and strong, inclined serifs
resembling the Venetian. Named after the sixteenth-century Italian
writing master Palatino, this type is highly legible and
has retained the aesthetic sculptural
form of the Venetian letter.

Type was set in Canada by Cooper & Beatty, Limited

Printed and bound in England by
Balding + Mansell Limited, Wisbech and London

The drawings on pages preceding the plates were reproduced from J. F. Lansdowne's preliminary sketches.